MW01505657

Two Kinds of Love

Two Kinds of Love

MARTIN LUTHER'S RELIGIOUS WORLD

Tuomo Mannermaa

Translated, Edited, and Introduced
by Kirsi I. Stjerna

With an Afterword
by Juhani Forsberg

FORTRESS PRESS
MINNEAPOLIS

TWO KINDS OF LOVE
Martin Luther's Religious World

First Fortress Press edition 2010

Translated and edited from the Finnish *Kaksi rakkautta: Johdatus Lutherin uskonmaailmaan* (Porvoo, Helsinki, Juva: WSOY, 1983).

Translation copyright © 2010 Fortress Press, an imprint of Augsburg Fortress. All rights reserved. Except for brief quotations in critical articles or reviews, no part of this book may be reproduced in any manner without prior written permission from the publisher. Visit http://www.augsburgfortress.org/copyrights/ or write to Permissions, Augsburg Fortress, Box 1209, Minneapolis, MN 55440.

Except in extracts from Luther's Works or unless otherwise noted, Scripture quotations are taken from the *New Revised Standard Version Bible*, copyright © 1989 by the Division of Christian Education of the National Council of Churches of Christ in the USA. Used by permission. All rights reserved.

Cover image: Martin Luther by Lucas Cranach
Cover design: Joe Vaughan
Book design: Michelle L. N. Cook

Library of Congress Cataloging-in-Publication Data
Mannermaa, Tuomo.
 [Kaksi rakkautta. English]
Two kinds of love: Martin Luther's religious world / Tuomo Mannermaa; translated, edited, and introduced by Kirsi I. Stjerna; with an afterword by Juhani Forsberg.—1st Fortress Press ed.
  p. cm.
Includes bibliographical references (p. 105) and index.
ISBN 978-0-8006-9707-5 (alk. paper)
1. Luther, Martin, 1483-1546. I. Stjerna, Kirsi Irmeli, 1963- II. Title.
BR333.3.M3613 2010
231'.6—dc22   2010009782

"The Study of the Fundamentals of Martin Luther's Theology in the Light of Ecumenism," Mannermaa's own reflection on how and where he places his most important findings ecumenically and philosophically is available at www.fortresspress.com/mannermaa.

The paper used in this publication meets the minimum requirements of American National Standard for Information Sciences — Permanence of Paper for Printed Library Materials, ANSI Z329.48-1984.

Manufactured in the U.S.A.

14   13   12   11   10   1   2   3   4   5   6   7   8   9   10

Contents

For Kirsi and Juhani

Abbreviations

CG   Thomas Aquinas, *Summa contra Gentiles*

LW   Luther's Works—American Edition. 55 Vols. Ed. Jaroslav Pelikan and Helmut T. Lehmann. St. Louis, Mo. and Minneapolis: Concordia Publishing House and Fortress Press, 2002.

Sta   *Studienausgabe* 1. Berlin: Van H. U. Delius, 1979.

Sth   Thomas Aquinas, *Summa Theologiae*

ThR   *Theologische Rundschau*

WA   D. Martin Luthers Werke: Kritische Gesamtausgabe. 67 Vols. Ed. J. K. F. Knaake et al. Weimar: H. Böhlau, 1883–1997.

WADB   D. Martin Luthers Werke. Kritische Gesamtausgabe. Deutsche Bibel. 12 Vols. Ed. P. Pietsch et al. Weimar: H. Böhlau, 1906–1961.

Editor's Introduction

It is a privilege and a joy to assist in making available another groundbreaking work of Professor Tuomo Mannermaa to an English-reading global audience. Both chronologically and thematically, this translation follows the English edition of Mannermaa's work, *Christ Present in Faith: Luther's View of Justification*, also by Fortress Press (2005), just as the Finnish originals did. Both Finnish books were quickly adopted as textbooks in Finnish theological education and discourse and have remained as pillars in Luther scholarship in Finland. Since their translation into German and through presentations in academic gatherings and the ensuing multilingual publications by a new generation of Finnish Luther scholars following in his footsteps, Mannermaa's vision and approach to Luther has become recognized internationally in its own right as unique—and controversial.

It is quite appropriate to talk about the "Mannermaa school." This is so because of the influence he has had in the formation of a group of scholars who continue to develop and test a particular methodological approach and line of argument, because of his stated challenge of earlier schools of thought in the interpretation of Luther (mostly German based), and, most importantly, because of the central arguments he has formulated about what is at the heart of Luther's theology and the identification of a key to understanding Luther's theology to its fullest.

While his thesis has been vividly discussed around the globe, and increasingly also so in North America, having his own voice through his original work available in English is long overdue. Not only of interest for scholars, Mannermaa's work has, as it were, removed a veil from Luther and his world of faith and thus made

Luther the spiritual teacher more approachable for contemporary seekers beyond denominational divides. Luther the teacher of faith has emerged in a new light and with a powerful perspective on the human-God relationship and on the foundations of Christian life that a contemporary person with spiritual concerns will find relevant, and this in an ecumenical context. (One example of this potential is the work of another Finn, Veli-Matti Kärkkäinen, from Fuller Theological Seminary, who is successfully applying the paradigm shifts evoked by the Finnish perspectives in current ecumenical discussions.)

Mannermaa's earlier book, *Christ Present in Faith*, provoked a good deal of excitement, and it will be interesting to observe the conversation that this volume will generate. The volume at hand gets further at the heart of the underappreciated yet central concept in Luther's faith system and theology, namely, love. Luther's theology or spirituality cannot be fully understood without delving into his understanding of love. Luther, in Mannermaa's treatment here, emerges as a unique theologian of love. His most central theological paradigms, such as the theology of the cross, justification by faith and salvation by grace, and *deus absconditus*, can only be understood wholly and to their fullest when set in the framework of the theology of love. Love, not "faith alone," is the actual key to understanding Luther's entire theology; faith without love remains an abstract principle in Luther's thinking. This is clearly a radical departure from the traditional Lutheran dialectic, with its distinctively different emphasis from that of the medieval theologians' prioritizing of love in relation to faith.

Mannermaa draws his arguments from Luther's own work, tracking his developing ideas from the earliest days of the reformer's career. Already in his Heidelberg Disputation (1518) Luther defined true theology as the theology of the cross, which, in his treatment, is ultimately the theology of love. In contrast to the vain and fallacious theology of glory—theology that looks for God in all the wrong places without recognizing that the appearance of God in God's full glory would be inconceivable and unbearable to human beings who can only expect to see the backside of God—the theology of the cross appreciates the unfathomable, that God surprises us in God's radical and incomprehensible love for us feeble-in-ourselves unlovable creatures, who continuously fail to see or respond to God's creative life-giving love with the right kind of love. Divine life needs to be given, and is given, to those whom God first loves. Luther concludes that God loves us sinners not because we deserve it or are lovable but in order to make us lovable, which is God's utmost desire. God's love creates, redeems, and sustains, without ceasing. In that "radiation therapy," we receive godly love—because of Christ's love, which we can believe with the faith that saves, the faith that also comes from God in Christ. Christ coming to us in grace, in all fullness, means a transformation and a new force that fills our beings and thus enables us to enter a relationship of love with our creator and fellow creatures, just as God has designed. Christ is the subject of that love, God's Love. In that love, we can experience oneness with God. Justification by faith—understood by Luther as our being made right with God and filled with God, becoming forgiven and fortified because of Christ, becoming full of God and transformed by God's love—can thus be most fully understood from the perspective of love. Being loved and becoming beloved and loving is at the heart of justification.

Understanding Luther as a theologian of love is a fresh approach to the old reformer. Mannermaa has broadened the profile of Luther already for decades and has pointed out obvious gaps in scholarship in this regard. When setting Luther's understanding of God's Love and Human Love in the late medieval context and in comparing his approach to the teaching of the leading medieval theologian, Thomas Aquinas, Mannermaa found a way to reexamine what exactly divided the reformer and his conversation partners. Where exactly did Luther's theology of the grace-filled and grace-based God-human relationship differ from his medieval counterparts and the tradition he was imbedded in? What in the medieval teaching of love did Luther actually criticize and what did he propose instead? These questions have value not only in deepening our understanding of Luther but also in promoting ecumenical work between Lutheran and Roman Catholic conversation partners. This exercise also brings Luther into conversation with some of the influential (yet overlooked in Lutheran tradition) teachers in Christian history, the mystics, in whose works the experience and idea of love had been central. In Mannermaa's treatment of Luther as a theologian of love, the reformer begins to look a lot like the mystics from whom Lutheran theologians traditionally have tried to disassociate themselves and "their" Luther.

Looking at the idea of love in Luther's theology, and appraising his teaching of the oneness in Christ in justification from that angle, we can indeed encounter the mystical heart of Luther. This recognition suggests significant continuities in the concerns and ultimate goals of the mystics and the reformer who was, after all, heavily influenced by late medieval mysticism, such as *devotio moderna* and the *German Theology* (the work he himself edited and translated). This reestablished connection is most exciting and one of the inspiring areas for new research bubbling among Luther scholars with respect to academic discourse as well as to new appraisals of Lutheran spirituality. Mannermaa's contribution here is palpable.

With Mannermaa's interpretation, we are beginning to view Luther from a new angle. Have we finally found the "real" Luther and what made him tick? Is Mannermaa correct in proposing that the "real Luther" is a theologian of love?

Mannermaa has made the weighty point that Luther has been much misunderstood in the past, that we have interpreted him too one-sidedly, for instance, when by-passing too quickly his theology of love as simply the criticism of the medieval concept of love and the model of salvation in which love played a central role in the greater "order" of things. While criticizing the view of salvation according to which a human being was to be shaped and reformed by love and grace with expectation of progressing in that relationship, Luther did not discard the concept of love entirely. Quite the contrary: he transformed it.

Mannermaa's thesis proves that we have left in the shadows the image of Luther as a teacher of faith, a teacher with a voice beyond denominational divides. The passion for Christians through the centuries has been the search to know God and for a personal relationship with God. Intimacy and unity with God are themes that Christian writers have explored consistently through centuries, with different visions for what we can expect from God in this life and the life to come, and what our options are in this regard. Luther shared these concerns and offered a vision much more radical than that of the dominant confessional Lutheran teachings. He boldly envisioned magnificent things to be in store for those loved by God and loving God. Oneness with Christ, the full presence of the Holy Spirit, godly life, and with that, the call to love as Christ loved, thus transforming the world with God's love. (The latter leads us to the area typically referred to as sanctification, a concept that Lutheran theology has had some difficulty with, even if it has definitely its own place in Luther's vision for the life of the justified.)

The underlying problem, Mannermaa claims, is the distorted history of interpretation. As already noted in *Christ Present in Faith*, Lutheran theology has been dominated by the different emphasis of the sixteenth-century confessional texts and their distinctively German interpretive tradition, which has shaped the conversations on the most central Lutheran doctrine, that of justification. Regardless of the stated primary authority of Luther concerning the doctrine of justification (as stated in the Formula of Concord), the confessional Lutheran teaching after Luther came to favor the "forensic" side of justification and its "declarative nature." Disagreeing with that emphasis, Mannermaa lifts up the place of the "effective" dimen- sion of justification in Luther's own articulation. He thereby opens a new vista on justification as real oneness with God, with a radical Christ-centered holiness beyond human achievement or effort. Try- ing to explain this through the concept of faith alone is difficult, if not unsatisfactory; taking the concept of love as the basis, the "effective" side of justification opens up with more ease and leads to a more holistic perspective on the God-human relationship and the Christian life. This, and much more, Mannermaa invites us to ponder with this focused reflection on the basics of Luther's theology of love and its place in his doctrine of justification, and vice versa.

Concerning the work of translating and editing: With Mannermaa's approval, I have tried to make the translation as clear and accessible as possible for English-speaking readers in particular. Other individuals have participated in this process in its earliest stages, and many have contributed in conversation and encouragement. It has been a joy and a delight to translate the often mysterious

Finnish expressions into English. For any strangeness in the translation, I bear full responsibility, while asking for the readers' kind consideration of the fact that the author did not write or think in English. Especially with the translation of the more philosophical terms, where the nuances are weighty and the translation choices riskier than in straightforward narratives, the primary concern has been clarity and original intention, rather than the convention of any "school" or tradition about the use of particular terms. Throughout the work, the goal was to preserve Mannermaa's own voice and style of articulating, preserving as much as possible the idiosyncratic expressions of the original language of the work, without compromising clarity. Some of the concepts have been difficult to translate satisfactorily into English, for example, the terms "essence" and "being," and the expressions "what is" and "what is not." Decisions regarding these terms have been explained in the notes. Moreover, to better emphasize Mannermaa's main argument about the distinction between God's love and human beings' love, the Finnish terms "Jumalan rakkaus" and "Ihmisen rakkaus" have been translated and capitalized as "God's Love" and "Human Love," even if that is not strictly following the grammar in the original Luther texts or in Mannermaa's text.

Translations of Luther's Latin and German texts that were not available in Luther's Works, American Edition, at the time of writing the book are from the author and the translator, while the translation in Luther's Works has been incorporated whenever possible (even if at times with occasional revisions, as indicated in the respective notes). A graduate student from Lutheran Theological Seminary at Gettysburg, Matthew Finney, assisted in the end by checking the English quotations (sponsored by the Institute for Luther Studies at that seminary). The notes with the text references have been preserved in their original form as much as possible, with some stylistic changes for consistency's sake and to be in line with the other works from Fortress Press. As requested by the publisher, quotations from the Bible, except for those from Luther's Works, are from the *New Revised Standard Version*. Here and there an editorial note is offered to explain a word choice or to offer a further clarification as needed.

The issue of inclusive language has been dealt with here as follows: While the author of this work and its translator and editor both embrace the principles of inclusive language (and naturally so as the Finnish native tongue does not distinguish between "he" and "she" in generic contexts, even if plagued with male-centered imagery for God, just as in other languages), it would have been cumbersome to make appropriate changes into all the quoted already existing Luther translations used in this work. Besides, Luther's own German or Latin often includes a certain amount of masculine language. In most cases, I have let the translations used reflect that reality, hoping that the reader can read these quotations with an enlightened mind and realize that the text is speaking of and to both sexes, while being confined within the conventions of the time and its language. The same applies to the citations from Luther's Works and their use of masculine words with respect to God, even when the original does not always warrant that. Occasionally, when I considered the exclusive and unnecessary use of "he" or "He" as simply too distracting, I have taken liberties to mildly revise the existing translation (always flagged in the respective note). The issue of inclusive language is too large to try to remedy in this single work where the attention is elsewhere and which comes from a context where the battles for inclusive language are quite different.

The afterword for this book comes from Dr. Juhani Forsberg, who is a long-term friend and colleague of Dr. Mannermaa and one of the pillars in Luther scholarship in Finland and in the training of new theologians. Continuously involved in scholarship and ecumenical work in particular, he has been a principal interpreter of the Finnish Luther school's efforts in Europe. In 2005 he published an article in the *Luther-Jahrbuch*, offering a substantial review of the most significant works on Luther produced by Finnish scholars from the time of the early stages of Mannermaa's work and that stem from the original stimulus from Mannermaa in one way or the other. The article makes known several foundational works on Luther that are not yet known to the international audience due to their language, Finnish or German. Here the article is offered in a much abbreviated and edited translation. For the full text, the readers can consult the German original "Die finnische Lutherforschung seit 1979" in *Luther-Jahrbuch* (2005), 147–82.

Finally, for further reading on Mannermaa's own reflection on how and where he places his most important findings ecumenically and philosophically, a short but very significant presentation from Mannermaa is available at www.fortresspress.com/mannermaa. "The Study of the Fundamentals of Martin Luther's Theology in the Light of Ecumenism" is especially important because of its attention to hermeneutical issues and in its explicit critical assessment of other schools of interpretation in light of which Mannermaa's thesis has been received.

On a personal note, it was in the 1980s when I had the delight to participate in the Luther seminar for systematic and ecumenical theology, a thesis seminar led by Dr. Mannermaa and Dr. Forsberg. The buzz around campus was that something extraordinary and special was taking place in that discipline of study. Many a budding scholar gravitated toward the study of ecumenics and ecumenical theology during those years—amid all the fascinating theological disciplines—because of the fresh perspectives explored with an "old" beloved topic, Martin Luther. Thirty years later, looking at the evidence in the ensuing works and broadened perspectives and introduction of new paradigms and renewed interest in wrestling with Luther the man of faith, we can attest that, yes, indeed, an entire new wave in Luther studies was taking wind then, and that wave continues to move forward with an increasing power, now across the continents, with this publication as a compass.

An important partner in supporting the publication of this work has been my home institution, the Lutheran Theological Seminary at Gettysburg, with its A. R. Wentz library, and in particular the Institute for Luther Studies, which has now for four decades promoted original Luther scholarship in the form of public lectures and publications. While not published officially in the "Encounters with Luther" (the publication of the annual Luther Colloquy lectures, now via Seminary Ridge Review), Mannermaa's book continues the venerable mission of fostering encounters with Luther across the continents and over language barriers. In many ways, Dr. Mannermaa and his interpretation have been an important part of the scholarly conversations on our campus and beyond and in the theological education of Lutheran seminarians, who will here gain yet another thought-provoking textbook.

Many thanks to the kind and wise people at Fortress Press. To Susan Johnson and Michael West, for their efforts to make available spirited works for their appreciative audience, and to Marshall Johnson for copyediting this work so beautifully. Heartfelt thanks to my family, especially my spouse and colleague, Brooks Schramm, for indulging me with windows of opportunity to participate in such an important and meaningful work as this.

Thank you, Juhani, for all you have done over the years and especially with this project, and for providing the review of the Finnish works on Luther. Thank you for trusting me to "knead" your words into English. This would be a good opportunity to say what is well known by many: your labors go beyond what can be mentioned in a brief thank you. Inkeri, Mrs. Mannermaa, let us express to you our warmest thanks for delivering messages over the years and all the things you do behind the scenes.

Thank you, Tuomo, for trusting me with your words. I hope I have done you justice. Let my labors for the rebirthing of this work be my sincere "thank you" for teaching me.

1. Love for "What Is" and Love for "What Is Not"

On April 26, 1518, a disputation was held in Heidelberg. In the aftermath of the turmoil caused by Martin Luther's Ninety-five Theses, Luther had been called to present his ideas in front of his peers, the Augustinian monks. For this occasion, Luther presented his theological arguments in the so-called Heidelberg Disputation, in which he outlined the basic structure of his new theology in twenty-eight theses. The content of these theses, according to Luther himself, can be called a "theology of paradoxes" (*theologia paradoxa*).[1] The very last of the theses, the twenty-eighth, holds the key to unlock the main idea presented in this disputation as a whole; as the climax of the theses, thesis 28 holds the key to unfold the essential and consistent meaning of the preceding theses.

According to Luther's arguments in the Heidelberg Disputation, there are two kinds of love: God's Love, that is, the love with which God loves, and Human Love, the love with which human beings love.[2] Luther formulates the difference between these two as follows: "God's Love does not find, but creates, that which is lovable (*diligibile*) to it. Human Love comes into being through that which is lovable to it."[3] In other words, God's Love is directed toward that which is empty and nothing, in order to create something of it and to make it exist in the first place. God's Love does not find in its object what makes it lovable but rather creates it. Human Love, by contrast, turns itself or is oriented toward that which already "is" something in itself and as such is good and beautiful. Indeed, Human Love comes into being on the basis of the prestige and glory of the one that is loved.

1

When defending his argument that Human Love comes into existence on the basis of the object of love, that is, from the object that is worth loving, Luther reminds his readers of the argument held by (in his opinion) "all" philosophers and theologians that the cause of love is always in its object. The faculties of human beings' mind and soul are always necessarily oriented and inclined toward external reality as their goal. For the intellect, the dimension of reality that one is aspiring to is real (*verum*), and for the will, or love, that dimension is good (*bonum*) and beautiful (*pulchrum*). The object for both human intellect and love is always something that already is, as something real. On this basis, Luther states that Human Love always finds its objects rather than creates them. Neither human knowledge nor human love can, by their nature, have as their objects something that is nothing, or that is empty, or that is evil or bad. The object of human knowledge and will, that is, the object of Human Love can only be something that already "is" and that as such is true, good, and beautiful. Therefore, human beings can neither love nor comprehend that which is not "something," nor that which is worthless or evil or "what is not." In Luther's view, this insight can be drawn from Psalm 41:1: "Blessed is the one who considers the poor and needy."⁴ Because Human Love comes into existence from its object, it receives goodness from its object rather than giving goodness to its object. In other words, human beings always seek their own, that is, their own good, in the objects of their love. At the same time this Human Love, by its nature, values that which "is" and is "something" and thus is precious and prestigious, both in the eyes of the one who loves and in the eyes of other human beings. This means that Human Love makes judgments from the face value regarding whom and what to love, rejecting some objects while accepting others.

By its very nature, Human Love cannot orient or turn itself toward that which is empty or evil, whereas God's Love by its very nature is just the contrary. God's Love is not oriented toward "what is" but rather toward "what is not." That is why God's Love does not desire to gain something good from its object but rather pours out good and shares its own goodness with its object. The cause for

God's Love thus is not outside the loving subject or something valuable in the object itself, but the cause of God's Love is the pure, creating, and giving goodness of the love itself. God's being, or essence,[5] itself is the incessant extroverted bubbling love that springs forth. Just as God has created everything out of nothingness and caused what is not or what does not exist to come into existence—to be—in the same fashion God's Love calls its beloved out of nothingness and surrounds its object with its own goodness and good things. These goods consist of all the gifts of God's creation given for the benefit of humankind. God's creating love is especially manifest when God— and those human beings in whom God's Love dwells—loves the sinners who are wicked, foolish, and weak, in order to make them righteous, good, wise, and strong. Luther crystallizes his idea of the love that creates as follows: "Therefore sinners are beautiful because they are loved; they are not loved because they are beautiful."[6] Furthermore, God's Love and Human Love result in two different ways of relating to the inequality among people. Because God's Love does not find but creates that which is lovable to it, it is not determined by the attributes of its object. It does not choose its object on the basis of these attributes, nor does it depend on human opinions, according to which the object of love always should be something. In principle, it turns or directs itself toward everything and everybody, paying equal attention to all. "He makes his sun rise on the evil and on the good" (Matt. 5:45).

The movements of God's Love and Human Love are polar opposites. The direction of Human Love is upwards, that is, it turns toward what is grand, wise, alive, beautiful, and good. God's Love, in turn, turns itself or is oriented downward, that is, toward what is lowly, disgraceful, weak, foolish, wicked, and dead. Therefore, God's Love irresistibly involves emptying oneself, suffering, and loving the cross. Even while dwelling in human beings, this kind of love knows the cross and is born of the cross. Luther says, "This is the love of the cross, born of the cross, which turns in the direction where it does not find good which it may enjoy, but where it may confer good upon the bad and needy person."[7]

Luther characterizes these two basic types of love by commenting on their two opposite directions. In *The Magnificat* Luther begins with the idea that it is in God's essence or being to always create something out of nothing. We could visualize this as follows: God always looks down into the abyss.

> Just as God in the beginning of creation made the world out of nothing, whence God is called the Creator and the Almighty, so God's manner of working continues unchanged. Even now and to the end of the world, all God's works are such that out of that which is nothing, worthless, despised, wretched, and dead, God makes that which is something, precious, honorable, blessed, and living. On the other hand, whatever is something, precious, honorable, blessed, and living, God makes to be nothing, worthless, despised, wretched, and dying. In this manner no creature can work; no creature can produce anything out of nothing. Therefore God's eyes look only into the depths, not to the heights; as it is said in Daniel 3:55 (Vulgate): "Thou sittest upon the cherubim and beholdest the depths."[8]

Similarly, Luther characterizes Human Love from its normal direction: Human beings look only upward and to the opposite of the abyss where poverty, anguish, and death prevail:

> The eyes of the world and men, on the contrary, look only above them and are lifted up with pride, as it is said in Proverbs 30:13: "There is a people whose eyes are lofty, and their eyelids lifted up on high." This we experience every day. Everyone strives after that which is above him, after honor, power, wealth, knowledge, a life of ease, and whatever is lofty and great. And where such people are, there are many hangers-on; all the world gathers round them, gladly yields them service, and would be at their side and share in their exaltation. Therefore it is not without reason that the Scriptures describe so few kings and rulers who were godly men. On the other hand, no one is willing to look into the depths where is poverty, disgrace, squalor, misery, and anguish. From these all turn away their eyes. Where there are such people, everyone takes to his heels, forsakes and shuns and leaves them to themselves; no one dreams of helping them or of making something out of

them. And so they must remain in the depths and in their low and despised condition. There is among men no creator who would make something out of nothing, although that is what St. Paul teaches in Romans 12:16 when he says, "Dear brethren, set not your mind on high things, but go along with the lowly."[9]

This radical difference between the descending God's Love and the ascending Human Love, something Luther insists on, raises the question if these two forms of love are totally mutually exclusive. At the same time, we need to ask whether Human Love, as opposite to God's Love, is evil, and whether its objects then are forbidden. Is Luther rejecting all kinds of Human Love and the values that can kindle it?

First, with this question in mind, we must pay attention to the "prefix" or a descriptive that Luther sets for his thesis about the different kinds of love. Luther uses a poignantly paradoxical manner of expression. "Paradox" is a rhetorical device or boost to increase the effect of a statement by expressing the idea in a way "contrary to what it seems" (Greek: *paradoxos*), or contrary to a generally held view, or contrary to the rules of logic. The meaning of "paradox" comes actually close to that of a "miracle." The purpose is to make the presented idea absolutely clear to the listeners through the use of the most sharply used opposites.

Paradox

Second, it should be noted that Luther also uses another rhetorical device familiar to him, namely, synecdoche. This mode of expression means that of the mutually related things at stake one is chosen to represent another, or that one aspect or part is chosen to represent the whole. Luther sees this rhetorical device being frequently used in Scripture.[10] In the same fashion, then, when speaking of Human Love, Luther uses one of its fundamental qualities in order to describe all human love (that is, he takes a part to present the whole). The quality he lifts up is the self-seeking orientation of Human Love toward that which exists, "what is," and that which is precious. Luther is not saying that a human being could never love with God's Love—after all, that is the very goal of all Christian faith—or that all human loving is the kind of Human Love he describes as opposite to God's Love. The thesis that "human beings

Synecdoche

seek their own good in all human loving that has as its object that which is something and that which is great" is not a synecdoche, whereas it is a synecdoche to say that all human love is always and exclusively this kind of self-seeking love. When speaking of Human Love, Luther uses one of the attributes to describe the whole. In so doing, he wants to emphasize, as strongly as possible, the significance of self-interested seeking for one's own in any form of human love, and especially so in the relationship between God and the human being.

Third, Luther neither denies the goodness of love nor implies that the objects of love would not be also God's good gifts for which human beings should give God praise. Luther does not belittle the love between a man and a woman. Quite the contrary, he speaks also of the physical side of such love as a gift of God more poignantly than any other theologian before him.[11] Nor does Luther deny the value of friendship love; after all, human beings are "naturally suited for a civilized and social existence."[12] Last but not least, Luther does not deny the importance and value of the love between parents and children, or people's love for animals, etc. The precious things that human beings love naturally are really and truly good gifts of God: only their evil or wicked use is what is wicked and evil or bad. With the concept Human Love, as in contrast to God's Love, Luther describes how a distorted seeking of one's own benefit is at work in the human loving that in itself is good. Human beings seek their own good both in their love for God and in their love for others. God's Love, however, opens the hearts of human beings, so that they can begin to love God without self-interest. At the same time, God's Love opens their eyes to see the real needs of their neighbors and to seek the good and the benefit of their fellow human beings. In other words, God's Love helps human beings first of all to love God as God and not only the goodness received from God, and, second, to love other human beings for themselves and as persons, instead of loving only their precious qualities and for what could be gained from them for the benefit of the one who loves.

This paradoxically presented distinction between two kinds of love constitutes the basic structure for the content of the Heidelberg Disputation. Even if the distinction between the two loves is actually explicated only in the very last of the theological theses, the differentiation between the two is at least implicitly present in the other theses as well. In fact, what is said (above) about the Heidelberg Disputation applies actually to all of Luther's works. The perspective of two kinds of love offers a most fruitful approach to the reformer's entire theology.

2. Two Kinds of Love and Love as a Unifying Power

The distinction between Human Love and God's Love (as defined in the previous chapter) determines the basic structure of Luther's theology. We can analyze this distinction further by focusing our attention on the question of how the classical understanding of love as a unifying power (*vis unitiva*)—that is, a movement that leads to a union (*unio*) or unification between the lover and the beloved—can be understood on the basis of these two kinds of love.[1]

At first sight, it appears that only the love that Luther calls Human Love can be this kind of unifying power. This kind of love comes into existence when the good in the beloved (in the object of love) kindles in the lover (the one who loves) an appetitive[2] movement (a "motion"), the goal of which is to take into oneself this good, that is, to precisely unify the lover and the beloved. It would appear that for Luther, the principal shortcoming of or problem with Human Love has to do with the idea of union or unification. That is, if God's Love is understood on the basis of Human Love and specifically as a uniting or unifying power, then it follows by necessity that God and human beings could become united or unified in the realization of their relationship. This in turn could appear to lead into abolition of the basic difference between the Creator and the created beings, and, consequently, would totally distort one of the basic premises of Christian faith.

Any interpretation, however, that would suggest that the concept of union (*unio*) or unification in any way would separate Human Love and God's Love is fallacious. Both kinds of love are essentially unifying powers. What makes them distinct from each other is not the idea of union or unification as such, but how the actual unification is perceived in each case. What the union or unification involves within the framework of God's Love is something quite different from what it means in the context of Human Love. At the same time, both types of love entail the idea of a union or unification between the lover and the beloved. This matter has not been sufficiently recognized in the past study of the history of the Christian idea of love.[3]

Luther expresses sharp criticism of any interpretation of the so-called golden rule (Love your neighbor as yourself) that would read it to command human beings to love themselves first and on that basis hold this self-directed love as the basic form and root for all other loving.[4] Because this interpretation, criticized by Luther, can be found in the theology of Thomas Aquinas,[5] and because Luther himself classifies Thomas as a representative of the "erroneous" theology of human love, it is necessary here to characterize briefly Thomas's understanding of love and its unifying power. My goal is not to explicate Thomas's complex understanding of love in full and detail but only as far as it is necessary to understand from this a particular historical context for Luther's criticism. It may be, in light of recent research, that the differences between the two are actually less than had been previously imagined. This issue, and the question of whether Luther has understood Thomas correctly, and whether the gap between these two theologians really is as wide as Luther himself claims it to be, is for ecumenical research to tackle. In this study, which aims to offer an introduction to Luther's theology and his "world of faith,"[6] it is most important to examine how the reformer himself understood this difference.

According to Thomas, love in its most general sense is found in the inclination, appetite, tendency, or striving of each creature toward the good that is inherent and proper to it. In this sense, love is the structuring principle of all reality, where all the moving power is about love. Thomas quotes Dionysius the Areopagite: "It is from love of the good that all things do whatever they do."[7] According to Thomas, this inclination toward the good that fills and expands one's essence is the essence of love in the broadest sense of the word.[8] To use a modern expression, we might say that love is about self-realization, one's inclination and effort to actualize fully all of one's potentials.

Love manifests itself in different degrees in all levels of reality and being: in inanimate matter, in flora and fauna, in animals, in human beings, and in God. For instance, we can consider the particular kind of love of a plant, for instance, a tree's love and its striving toward its good. Naturally, Thomas points out, we must be careful not to regard the vegetative love of the plant as love in the fullest sense of the word. In its truest sense, love belongs to the personal reality of human beings. The example of the love of a tree, however, helps to illustrate some of the characteristics of all love, just as analyzing primitive cells assists in understanding the structures of more complicated organisms.

The first fact is that the seed of a tree exists, that is, it has its existence. Second, the seed has a particular essence (that is, exactly what the being is), which is oriented toward the specific good inherent to it, namely, the form of a flourishing tree. Out of this form of substance or substantial form arises a shaping force that drives the plant into a specific formative process. In other words, there is in the essence or substance of the seed a particular inclination or a drive toward the actualization of its substantial form, that is, toward the growth of the seed into a tree. The same idea can be expressed by saying that the actualized form of the tree is the good of the germinating seed and the growing tree, toward which it aims by its natural tendency—that is, when striving toward that which it loves.

While aiming toward this goal, the substantial form of the seed develops out of itself nonsubstantial forms and capacities—that is, accidental forms—which are separate yet related to its substance. The basic orientation of the plant's substantial form finds its actualization with the help of these capacities, among which are such accidental forms and capacities as the tree's roots, trunk, bark, branches, and leaves. All these are in the service of the total form or the "total good" as the plant is oriented toward, that is, as it loves those partial goods that are necessary for the plant to reach its end goal. The branches bend toward the sunlight; the light is their good. The roots turn toward water and minerals; they are the good that the roots aspire for, that is, what they love, and with which they unite. In a sense, we could say that in loving its own full form, or in trying to actualize it, the tree loves the sun, the air, the water and the minerals just as it loves itself, becoming unified with them. According to Thomas, the general essence of love is about the appetite or the desire of the lover to assimilate itself into the good that it loves; or, to express it differently, it is "a creature's orientation toward itself in its orientation toward the other." According to Thomas, all love follows a particular interpretation of the golden rule (Love your neighbor as yourself).[9]

The example of a tree already reveals some of the fundamental and general characteristics of love: love is an orientation and an inclination toward the good that is inherent to each creature, and it seeks to unite this good so closely to itself that the lover and the beloved become one. Furthermore, the example of the tree also makes obvious another point of essential importance to Luther's criticism: because love is about each being's orientation and inclination toward that which is inherent, that is, good, then it is always oriented toward what is, and never toward what is not. This becomes clear from the following line of thought: In comparison to a full-grown tree, the seed is a mere potentiality, whereas the full-grown tree with its full form is an actualized or realized potentiality. The latter exists as a tree, in comparison with the seed's not-yet-existence as a tree. Hence, love is always oriented toward "what is," and love is about each creature's self-realization, actualization of its very essence. The existence of each creature is about a single process of loving and uniting.

This example of a tree reveals yet another interesting point in regard to what Luther criticizes. In accordance with the logic of Thomas (who follows the Aristotelian line of thought), the movement with which any given being or creature, for instance, a seed, aims toward its goal, is an act or a work (*ergon*, work). It is through an act or a work that the tree loves or actualizes its own good, or—to use Luther's expression—becomes good.

We must be careful, however, not to try to fathom Thomas's entire teaching of love from the single example of a tree. The main significance of this example is to elucidate how love is an essential part of the prevalent orientation in all beings toward their own good or what is inherently good for them. According to Thomas, there are different kinds of orientations and thus different kinds of love. First, there is the mute and blind externally stimulated orientation or inclination of the inanimate beings toward their own good. Second, there is the vegetative orientation or inclination of plants. Third, there is the emerging sensitive orientation of animals. Fourth, and finally, there is the cognitive and intellectual orientation or inclination of human beings, namely, their will.[10]

The true essence of love can be understood only from the human being's personal reality. Admittedly, the mute love of the inanimate matter, as well as the vegetative love of plants and the sensitive love of animals are all included in human beings' love, where they become a new entirety, reshaped by human reason and will. As a whole, this new form of human orientation or inclination gives a new goal for the inanimate, vegetative, and sensitive orientation effective in human beings; it gives it the new form inherent to human beings and the equivalent love.[11]

All the levels of being thus become united and unified in human beings, who, in a way, are everything. Passion, for example, is an attribute of love that primarily belongs to the level of the sensitive soul, yet all human love can, in a sense, be about passion. Hence, the intellectual love of human beings can be passionate, just as sensitive passions can be guided by intellect.

Because all kinds of loving are unified into one entirety in human beings, we can choose one type of love that is characteristic to humanity in order to characterize all forms of love. Passionate love, because of its unambiguous nature, is most suitable for this purpose.[12] A prerequisite for passionate love is the existence of two realities that are opposite to each other. One of these poles is the emerging orientation in human beings toward some good; the other pole is the real and actual presence of this object. A relation filled with tension emerges between these two poles. An effect or an influence proceeds from the present good, the beloved, and engenders in the lover a movement toward the loved one. According to Thomas, love is precisely this motion toward the beloved, a movement caused by the loved one. When love is still on its way toward its goal, it is a form of longing or an appetite. What follows after the end of the motion, is rest or joy.[13] Because this kind of motion of love is engendered from the outside by attraction caused by the object of one's love, the beloved, love is then passion in the truest sense of the word: love is simultaneously about being under the influence—that is, suffering or passion— and also the most active form of spontaneous motion or movement. Within the circle of these mutual conditions of being the influence and being under the influence—that is, being the lover who acts and the beloved who is acted upon—passion can grow into an all-encompassing power.

In the concept of passionate, desiring love, we can see quite clearly the idea of similarity, which is at the basis of Thomas's understanding of love. This concept of similarity links the idea of love as orientation toward good and the idea of love as a unifying power. According to the notion of similarity, all creatures are reaching toward that which somehow corresponds with their essence and thus belongs to them.[14] An attractive or appealing or exciting effect proceeds from the object of the desire, and the lover reacts to it with pleasure, with a desire to participate in the object as the lover's own good. "This inner affective orientation, adaptation, or adjustment of the inclination to something as its 'own good' is called love." In other words, in its proper essence love is "having the same attitude toward another as toward oneself."[15]

It is clear that this definition of love as an orientation or inclination toward another as if toward oneself, a notion that is based on the idea of similarity, can in different contexts be given totally different moral meanings.

For example, when a human being loves or desires a precious object, we can say that the person's whole essence is in the object: one is relating to it as one relates toward oneself. Here we have, according to Thomas, the form of love that he calls lusting love or concupiscent love (*amor concupiscentiae*). In this form of love, the relation between the lover and the beloved is such that the lover lacks what the beloved has, and the lover wants to have for himself or herself that which he or she lacks. Thus, here the similarity consists of the similarity between what is lacking from the lover and what is found in its fullness in the beloved.[16]

One can relate toward another as if relating to oneself, however, in a manner that is entirely different, according to Thomas. As distinct from the concupiscent love, there is also benevolent love (*amor benevolentiae*), that is, friendship or love between friends or "love of friendship" (*amor amicitiae*). In friendship love, other human beings are loved as persons for their own sake, and not for the sake of anything to be gained from them. In friendship love one does not ask for good things for oneself, but "wills good" for the other.[17]

By distinguishing between concupiscent and friendship love, Thomas seeks to solve the much-debated problem in the Middle Ages about the relationship between "self-interested" and "not self-interested" love. This is not an easy task, because, according to Thomas's general definition, love is an inclination toward the actualization of each creature's inherent good. Would this definition of love then mean literally that all love is necessarily self-interested, that is, love of one's self?

Once again, the solution to this problem draws from the concepts of similarity and union or unification. According to Thomas's interpretation of the golden rule, love means having the same attitude toward another as toward oneself. This proper essence of love finds its best realization in friendship love, which is the highest form of human love.

In concupiscent, lusting love, that which is missing in the lover corresponds with that which is found in its fullness in the beloved. In other words, in concupiscent love the potentiality or the matter of the lover corresponds with the actuality or the form of the beloved. Friendship love, in turn, emerges when the lover and the beloved have a shared fullness and actuality, that is, a common form. Friendship is based on the fact that the friends have much in common and much actualized fullness to share, such as equal intelligence and level of education, and similar emotional sensitivity. In friendship love, the similarity and the union between the lover and the beloved actually extend so far that a friend is to a friend like another "I." For this reason, when the one who loves is wishing good to the beloved, he or she is simultaneously wanting good for himself or herself. The one who is giving is also receiving; reciprocal sharing of goods occurs.[18]

Hence, the nature of the friendship love as the love that does good to the other, instead of being concupiscent love, is based on the notion of similarity and union or unification. What is good for one of the two friends is good for the other as well. Moreover, when the lover wills good for the other, he or she receives good things as well. Thus, the essence of friendship is in the reciprocal sharing of goods from the shared fullness and richness, in the communication between the two, and thus in the mutual enrichment in the relationship. Only friendship love, then, is love in the proper sense of the word.

In this introduction to Luther's world of faith, it is not necessary to ponder whether Thomas's solution to the problem of "non-self-interested" love is, objectively speaking, appropriate. In order to understand Luther's criticism, the essential conclusion to observe is this: benevolent love (*amor benevolentiae*) or the friendship love (*amor amicitiae*) that Thomas describes is not the same in content as God's Love, which, according to Luther, is oriented toward "what is not" or that which is lacking, and evil. Thomas himself says it is not enough for friendship that one wants good things for the other, because friendship requires a mutual sharing of goods and reciprocal love: we are friends only to those who are our friends. Thomas says, "Goodwill alone is not enough for friendship, for this requires a mutual loving; it is only with a friend that a friend is friendly. But such reciprocal goodwill is based on something in common."[19]

Friendship love, thus, is no exception to the rule that love is always oriented toward "what is" and what is good. In accordance with this definition of the form of love, "what is" is loved as "itself," rather than as something "in relation to" something else, as is the case with desiring, concupiscent love.[20] Because even friendship love is oriented toward an object "that is," the difference between friendship love and concupiscent love, from Luther's perspective, is not as clear-cut as it may seem in Thomas's definition. Even friendship love follows the general rule for the nature of love, namely, that love is always about actualization of the inherent good of each being. Thus also friendship love is based on the "form" of the object of its orientation—the "form" referring here to "what is" and what is good, and what generates in human beings the inclination toward friendship love.[21]

At the same time, it becomes clear how consistently Thomas interprets the golden rule (Love your neighbor as yourself) in the very manner criticized by Luther. Thomas regards human beings' love for themselves—that is, their orientation toward the good that is prescribed to them by their own essence or being—as the root of all other forms of love, including friendship love that is without self-interest. It must be noted, however, that this love is not any form of crude love for one's self, but precisely the kind of love for one's self that God, according to Thomas, has planted in each creature's essence and nature, even with a command for each being to actualize its own good. Thomas writes about the relationship between benevolent friendship love and self-love:

> And here we must concede that, strictly speaking, we do not have friendship for ourselves, but something more, because friendship implies a union of some kind, love being, as Dionysius puts it, a unifying force, whereas, with regard to himself, man possesses unity, which is something more than union. Accordingly, as unity is presupposed to union, so our love for ourselves is the model and root of friendship; for our friendship for others consists precisely in the fact that our attitude to them is the same as to ourselves. Aristotle remarks that friendly feelings towards others flow from a man's own feelings towards himself.[22]

Thomas, then, teaches that because love is each creature's inclination and orientation toward its own inherent good, human beings love this inherent good as they love themselves. Love is a unifying power precisely in the sense that loving is, in a way, relating to one's self in relating to the other; that is, the unifying power is each creature's own orientation and inclination toward its own good and self-realization. Because Thomas Aquinas teaches that each being's self-realization is based on its love for itself, love for self is then the model and root of all love. As the commentator in the German edition of *Summa Theologiae* says:

> Quite universally, the fact that two certain essences factually have this orientation toward each other, that is, belong somehow

together and are akin to each other, relies on the unity that prevails between the two poles, and without which no love is possible. Somehow the lover seeks and rediscovers himself in the other and wills good for the other as for his own self, when the love concerned is love that deserves its name without restrictions. Thus, we have already referred to the fact that it is just natural and necessary that love for self must appear first, because the human being has the closest bonds with himself, or belongs first to himself in his own individual unity; because of his love for himself there is an inherent drive in him toward the enrichment and realization of his own being. Moreover, love for self is the very root out of which all other kinds of love (love for God as well as love for one's neighbor) grow, and it is to be the guideline for all the other kinds of love: "You shall love your neighbor as yourself."[23]

Luther admits that the concept of love described above is an apt portrayal of natural reality, but he denies its suitability as a fundamental model for Christian ethics. Primarily, however, Luther criticizes Thomas for making the kind of love that turns toward the good and toward "what is" also the basis for interpreting God's love. Thomas interprets both God's love for human beings and human beings' love for God through the concept of self-realizing love. According to Luther, it is not until this point that an actual error occurs. All the distortions of Christian faith criticized by Luther seem to be consequences of this fundamental presupposition that makes Human Love the premise for interpreting human beings' relationship with God as well.

Thus even God's self-love is regarded by Thomas as a kind of self-realizing love. Even God loves the good that is inherent and proper to God. Because God is the most perfect being, in whom all the potentialities and all the goods have already become realized—after all, God is the most "real" being and the highest good—then the first object of God's love can only be God's own being and essence. Expressed in Christian trinitarian language: within the Holy Trinity, the inner love of the Holy Trinity loves another in the most perfect way when loving itself, which means that God the Trinity "is" the perfect friendship love.[24] Thus the interpretation of the golden rule through the pattern of self-realization is extended analogically even to Godself. This basic definition of God's love has many consequences and is central for understanding Luther's criticism of Thomas.

The first consequence of this interpretation of Thomas, according to which God's love follows, in a certain sense, the model of self-realizing love (or, to be more exact, the pattern of friendship love), is that God's love, just as all love, turns only toward that which is good. Nothing that is bad or evil can ever be an object of God's love in itself but can only be loved in relation to something good, in which case it is actually loved as something good. Because God is the highest good, God necessarily loves God's own essence and being more than anything else. In relation to things outside of Godself, God loves the object in proportion to the degree to which its proper goodness has become actualized. This leads to Thomas's proposition: God's love is always greater toward that which is better.[25]

Furthermore, Thomas's interpretation of God's love as self-realizing friendship love has another consequence closely connected with the previous one. God is not only the highest good but also the most "real" being, in whom all the potentialities of good are a reality, that is, in whom they exist. Thus, "being" and "good" are interchangeable concepts. From the principle that God loves God's own essence more than anything else, it follows that the primary object of God's love is God's "pure" existence. Therefore, in relating "outwardly" to its objects, God loves more those objects that are already "realized in being"; the more the objects are realized, the more God loves them. In other words, God always loves that which is something, whereas "what-is-not," or what is nothing, cannot be the object of God's love in any other way but in relation to something that already is; it, or they, can be loved as potentialities for something and, thus, as "being something."

This explains the historical background for Luther's argument that Human Love is always oriented toward what is good and "what is," and that its object can never be anything that "is not" or is evil or bad. Luther concludes that in scholastic theology, which follows the logic of Aristotle, the image of God has been changed into the likeness of the human image and human beings, and thus in accordance with Human Love.

Interpreting God's Love as love that realizes itself in a particular way has yet another fundamental consequence, which has to do with the idea of the created beings' love for God. Because God loves God's own essence and being as the highest good, all created beings have been created in the image of this particular pattern of love. In fact, each creature's striving toward the good that is proper or inherent to it—love, in other words—is a reflection of God's way of loving. Like God, all creatures love that which is good and "what is." Because God is the realization of all that is good, and because all the potentialities are a pure reality and actuality in God, therefore the proper good of all creatures, which they are always oriented toward in their self-realization, that is, their loving, is a potentiality that already exists as an actuality in God. From this follows an essential conclusion: in loving their inherent or proper good, creatures are unknowingly loving God. In other words, to love anything that is good is possible only in the horizon provided by good(ness) itself, God. For instance, even when an inanimate matter, a plant or an animal, loves the good proper or inherent to it, it unknowingly loves God. It is the duty of human beings, however, to love God intentionally and consciously.[26]

It must be noted, however, that Thomas does not consider human beings' relationship with God to be about self-interested love but in some fashion about friendship love. Because friendship is possible only between those who are like one another, and because God loves only that which is good, God must create in human beings a new and good form; this so-called created grace makes them worthy of friendship with God. The created grace is a new quality attached to the essence of human beings and gives them a new goal and, with it, a new movement toward the actual proper good of human beings— God. This movement is love, and Thomas calls it *caritas*, God's Love. Also this love follows the law characteristic of all love. Just as the form of a flourishing tree is somehow already present in the seed of a tree, in the same way *caritas* as God's love somehow already has its object, the essence of God, within itself.[27] Furthermore, according to Aristotle, the actualization or entelechy[28] of a motion (the state of already being in its destination) is reached through an act or a work (*ergon*) and, in like manner, *caritas*, the love of God, as a motion is an act or a work. Human beings are not saved on account of this act, or work, but they are nevertheless saved in these "acts", that is, in the loving movement toward the highest good or happiness, which is God.[29]

In order to avoid misunderstandings, it must be emphasized that according to Thomas, this *caritas* or love of God is given to human beings by grace alone. On this point Thomas and Luther speak the same language. As mentioned above, however, Luther mainly criticized the scholastic theology for interpreting human beings' relationship with God through the pattern of Human Love. Luther explicitly states that the scholastics learned their view of love from Aristotle. In other words, they interpreted the idea of *caritas* being infused by "grace alone" through a philosophical model. Hence, just as any creature's love was seen as a movement toward the good proper to it, and the actualization of this motion of entelechy (the state of already being in its destination) was regarded as an act or a work, in the same way *caritas* as a gift was seen as a movement toward God to be realized in various stages as a work toward God.

Thus, it is typical that in Thomas's thinking the progress of this movement of love toward God follows any law of movement: "We see the same kind of thing in the movement of a body, which first of all draws away from one point, then approaches, and finally comes to rest at another point."[30] According to this general law of motion, the growth of human beings' love for God begins, first, with their efforts to resist sin and the desires that are opposed to this love. From this follows, second, human beings' struggle to strengthen and fortify their love for God (*caritas*). Third, human beings aspire to unite with God and enjoy (*frui*) God as the highest goal. This is "characteristic of the perfect who long to depart and to be with Christ."[31]

What follows from the above-described view of the essence of the love of God (*caritas*) is a particular order of love given to human beings. First, the primary object of the love of each human being is he or she himself or herself, because God, the highest good, has become unified with that person. Second, the human being's love is oriented toward the neighbor as a fellow friend of God, that is, as an object of friendship love, and as an equal partaker of the divine riches. It should also be noted here that when loving another human being, the ultimate object or target of loving is God, the highest good. Third, love is oriented toward sinners. Sinners are loved, however, only insofar as they are human beings, that is, potentially able to participate in God. They are not loved insofar as they are sinners. From Luther's point of view, this order of love presented by Thomas consistently deals with the kind of love in which human beings always love what is good and "what is" and is thus something toward which they relate to as if to themselves.

The actual target of Luther's criticism is the interpretation in which human beings' relationship with God is understood through the concept of the self-realizing Human Love that is oriented toward "what is" and what is good. "Where they [the scholastics] speak of love, we speak of faith."[32] This statement of Luther entails the core of his reformation program. For Luther, faith is the fundamental concept that characterizes human beings' relationship with God, instead of appetitive desiring and self-realizing love; this faith means the reception of God's Love, which, first, turns "downward" toward "what is not" or toward nothingness and evil, and, second, has become flesh in Christ.

What Luther is essentially criticizing is the use of metaphysics based on Greek philosophy as a central interpretative principle for Christian faith. Luther's battle against scholastic metaphysics involves at least two major points. The first deals with the actual scholastics' concept of love, and the second with the underlying particular interpretation of the nature of human beings' knowledge of God.

1. First, Luther's criticism is directed against the scholastic theologians' understanding of Human Love and its characteristic interpretation of love as a unifying power. Special attention should be paid to Luther's argument that God's Love is also a unifying power, even if with the contrasting prefix or descriptive of that of Human Love. God's Love "turns in the direction where it does not find good which it may enjoy, but where it may confer good upon the bad and needy person."[33] This is the actual core difference between Luther and Thomas. According to Luther, God does not desire or love

that which has a form or being, that is, goodness, beauty, wisdom, power, and so forth. Rather, God's Love gives and unites that which is good—that is, form—to that which lacks form and is nothing in relation to goodness and form. God thus applies form to those who are deficient, sinful, evil, foolish and weak, in order to make them righteous, good, wise, and strong. In other words, God follows God's own manner of acting: creating something out of nothingness. "This is what it means to be God: Not to receive but to give good."[34] God realizes and actualizes God's essence—that is, God gives—first of all by bestowing existence upon all that exists. The creation as such, with all its goods, is a gift from God. Second, God gives God- self in Christ, that is, God applies God's form and goods to human beings, who lack form, who are deficient, ugly, and sinful. At the same time, Christ takes upon himself their needs, sin, and death, to bear as his own their deficiencies, needs, sins, and death. God unites with human beings really, truly. Love as a unifying power, then, is not merely about God's benevolent attitude toward human beings. Rather, God loves human beings by giving them Godself fully, that is, by giving them God's full "nature" with all of God's characteristics, such as righteousness, power, life, joy, and so forth. Faith receives the good deed of Christ, and the task of Christians is to love God and God's will without self-interest and to be Christ to their neighbors. This means, to do for their neighbors as Christ has done first for them: to give the good gifts they have received to their neighbors in need, and to relate to the neighbors' sins, weaknesses, and needs as if these were their own.[35] In this way, Christ, Christians, and their neighbors form one body in God and God's love.

Obviously, what lies behind Luther's interpretation of God's Love as a unifying power is his understanding of the golden rule (Love your neighbor as yourself). Differing from Thomas, in Luther's view the golden rule does not command human beings to love themselves first but regards their natural love for themselves as a self-evident fact. What the golden rule commands is that human beings consider the needs of their neighbors as important as they, sinfully, consider their own needs—that is, as absolutely impor- tant.[36] In other words, when human beings place themselves in the position of their neighbors, they can know (on the basis of their own example, both by their reason and affect) what others need and what they have to do in order to help others. In his exposition of the golden rule, Luther says as follows:

> Now this particular commandment provides you with a most living example, namely, yourself. Hence, this example is nobler than that of all the saints, because they have all passed away and died, whereas this particular example is alive. Namely, all human beings must admit that they can feel how they love themselves. They feel, indeed, how busy they are taking care of their own lives, how eager they are to foster their bodies with food, clothes and all that is good, and how they avoid death and all kinds of unhappiness. This is your love for yourself, and you can see it and feel it. What, then, is the moral of this commandment? It tells you to do [to your neighbor] exactly the same things which you do to yourself: you should let [your neighbor's] body and life be as important to you as are your own body and life. How could anyone have given you an example closer to you than this, or one more living and powerful? Or how could anyone have given you another example lying as deep inside you as this one—so deep, indeed, that it is actually yourself?"[37]

According to Luther, the golden rule represents the so-called natural law, which God has "drawn" in the hearts of all human beings, whether they are aware of it or obey it or not.[38] All ethical human activity, the Ten Commandments (the Decalogue), and the legal systems of societies are based on this rule and principle of placing oneself in the position of others.[39] Luther thinks, in fact, that even God obeys the golden rule, fulfilling the law when coming in Christ in the position of human beings, in order to take on their needs and wants.[40] Hence, not only Thomas, but also Luther teaches that the golden rule is the principle of interpretation for both Human Love and God's Love. In Luther's theology, however, the golden rule finds its content in the principle of God's Love: "This is what it means to be God: Not to take good but to give it." According to the golden rule as understood on the basis of God's Love, human beings are called to love God and their neighbors with a pure love without self-interest. On the one hand, human beings shall "place themselves in the position of God," that is, do what God expects from human beings whom God has created: let God be God, the good Giver of all the goods of creation and redemption. On the other hand, human beings are also called to "place themselves in the position of their neighbors," and to deliver to them good gifts of God in accordance with the neighbors' needs.

2. Second, Luther's criticism against scholastic metaphysics is directed not only toward its actual concept of love but also toward the premise that enables the scholastics to employ this metaphysical concept of love in their interpretation of Christian faith. In the theology criticized by Luther, it was taken for granted that human beings can comprehend the essence of God on the basis of created reality and also make the inner structure of created reality into the central principle for the interpretation of Christian faith. Luther is also of the opinion that in principle God's essence can generally be known through God's works of creation; however, human beings cannot reach this knowledge of God by merely observing God's works of creation if they ignore Christ. The "metaphysicians" forget the image of the cross (*imago crucis*), but for Luther, God is a hidden God, whose action is concealed within the paradox of the cross and in the negation of God's "attributes of glory."

3. The Theology of Glory versus the Theology of the Cross

There are two opposite kinds of theologies that are based on the difference between Human Love and God's Love: a theology of glory and a theology of the cross. The distinction between these two is pivotally important for understanding Luther's concept of faith. The theology of the cross is not just one article of faith among others but rather the essential content of all of Luther's faith statements. It is presupposed and implicitly stated even when not mentioned explicitly. In brief, the difference between the theology of glory and the theology of the cross is as follows: the theologian of glory looks "upward" and wishes to stare at the attributes of the majesty and glory of God—in other words, God's divinity. The theologian of the cross, in turn, looks "downward" and sees the image of the cross, looking at God in humanity, weakness, and folly.

In theses 19, 20, and 21 of the Heidelberg Disputation, the difference between the theology of glory and the theology of the cross is presented as follows:

[19.] That person does not deserve to be called a theologian who looks upon the invisible properties of God understood through the created things [Rom. 1:20]. This is apparent in the example of those who behaved in such a way and still were called fools by the Apostle in Rom. 1 [:22]. Furthermore, the invisible things of God are power, godliness, wisdom, justice, goodness, and so forth. The recognition of all these things does not make one worthy or wise.

[20.] One deserves to be called a theologian, however, who comprehends the visible and the "back" of God seen through suffering and the cross. The "back" and the visible things of God are opposites of the invisible, namely, human nature, weakness, foolishness. The Apostle in 1 Cor. 1 [:25] calls them the weakness and folly of God. Because human beings misused the knowledge of God through works, God wished again to be recognized in suffering, and to condemn wisdom concerning invisible things by means of wisdom concerning visible things, so that those who did not honor God as manifested in God's works should honor God as God is hidden in suffering. As the Apostle says in 1 Cor. 1 [:21], "For since, in the wisdom of God, the world did not know God through wisdom, it pleased God through the folly of what we preach to save those who believe." Now it is not sufficient for anyone, and it does one no good to recognize God in God's glory and majesty, unless one recognizes God in the humility and shame of the cross. Thus God destroys the wisdom of the wise, as Isa [45:15] says, "Truly, you are a God who hides yourself."

So, also, in John 14 [:8], where Philip spoke according to the theology of glory: "Show us the Father." Christ forthwith set aside his flighty thought about seeing God elsewhere and led him to himself, saying, "Philip, he who has seen me has seen the Father" [John 14:9]. For this reason true theology and recognition of God are in the crucified Christ. . . .

[21.] A theology of the glory calls evil good and good evil. A theology of the cross calls the thing what it actually is. This is clear: One who does not know Christ does not know God hidden in suffering. Therefore one prefers works to suffering, glory to the cross, strength to weakness, wisdom to folly, and, in general, good to evil.[1]

What lies behind the distinction between the theology of glory and the theology of the cross is Luther's concept of the two kinds of love: the theology of glory is based on Human Love, whereas the theology of the cross is based on God's Love.

It is typical of the theologians of glory not to hold the image of the cross before their eyes. It is in the cross, however, that God's Love manifests most clearly—God's Love that in itself is oriented downward, toward "what is not" or what is bad and evil. God has descended so far down to the position of human beings that God has even assumed the human form, their humanity, weakness, folly, sin, and hell, as if these were God's own. In so uniting with human beings, God bestows upon them God's own goods, namely, God's divine righteousness, power, wisdom, joy, and eternal life—in other words, God's own essence. Contrary to this, the theologians of the glory, in their attempt to reach and love God while bypassing the cross, seek God in God's great and impressive attributes. In other words, they seek God as an object of love that turns toward "what is" and is thus "something" and "good." Luther says:

> But the theologian of glory . . . learns from Aristotle that the object of the will is good and that good is to be loved and evil is to be hated. Therefore God is for him the highest good and the highest object of love.[2]

The theologian of glory infers from God's creation (the visible world) what invisible God is like. Luther comments on this: "That person does not deserve to be called a theologian who looks upon the invisible things of God understood through the created things."[3]

Indeed, it was thought in the so-called natural theology of the scholastics that God's essence could be known in three ways. (These are not the same as Thomas's five proofs for God's existence.) These three ways were (1) the way of estrangement, or way of distancing (*via remotionis*), (2) the way of attribution, or the way of uniting the qualities (*via attributionis*), and (3) the way of eminence, or the way of strengthening the qualities (*via eminentiae*). They were all based on the principle that the attributes that represent perfection in the created and visible reality can be magnified and multiplied to infinity when applied to the concept of God.[4] Thus, as befits the scheme of Human Love, the theologians of glory have fixed their gaze beyond the visible cross upon the invisible God of glory who is the infinite power, the infinite divinity, the infinite wisdom, the infinite righteousness, goodness, and so forth. According to Luther, "The recognition of all these things does not make one worthy or wise."

This fairly daring criticism is clearly based on the concept of God's Love. The theologians of glory, who love God as their highest good and as the most real being, cannot understand God who would be found in the "evilness" and "nothingness" of the cross. The reason and love of the theologians of glory—and of every human being, for that matter, as all human beings are naturally theologians of the glory—are directed only toward that which is "something" and which is good. In accordance with God's Love, the true God is where the objects of God's Love are—that is, in humanity, weakness, and folly. But as is typically the case, in the eyes of the theologians of glory—and human beings in general—the true God seems as if "nothing" or "evil."

This suggests to Luther that Thomas's Aristotelian concept of God is clearly a form of the theology of glory and elucidates in a particularly clear manner that which is common to every theology of glory. That is, theologies of glory view the essence of God within the framework of Human Love instead of God's Love. What Luther sees as the fundamental deficiency in the Aristotelian concept of God is the fact that it does not present God as a God for human beings, that is, as the God who loves human beings with God's Love. Luther says:

> For they have no other knowledge of God than a philosophical or metaphysical one, namely, that God is a being separate from the creatures, as Aristotle says—a being that is truthful and contemplates the creature within itself. But of what concern is this to us? The devil, too, has such a knowledge of God and knows that He is truthful. But when knowledge is imparted about God in theology, God must be known and apprehended, not as remaining within Himself but as coming to us from outside; that is, we must maintain that He is our God. That first Aristotelian or philosophical god is the god of the Jews, the Turks, and the papists; but he is of no concern to us.[5]

In contrast to the theologians of glory, the theologians of the cross fix their gaze upon the God who has come to us, and comprehend "the visible and manifest things of God seen through suffering and the cross" (LW; literally: "the visible things of God and the attributes of God's back seen through suffering and the cross"). In order to understand this passage, we must notice that the expression "the attributes of God's back" literally refers to God's back (*posteriora*). This phrase contains an allusion to the Latin version of Exodus 33 in the Vulgate, in which Moses asks God to show him God's glory. God answers that Moses will not be allowed to see God's face, "for no one shall see me and live" (Exod. 33:20). After this God says that God will put Moses in the cleft of a rock, and that Moses will be covered with God's hand until God's glory has passed by. "Then I will take away my hand, and you shall see my back; but my face shall not be seen."[6]

When we take into account what the expression "God's back" means, we can understand what is characteristic of the theologians of the cross in their relationship with God. First, they observe what can be seen of God from God's backside: God's humanity, weakness, and folly. Second, they look at these attributes of God through their own sufferings and cross, that is, through their own humanity, weakness, and folly. The cross of Christ and the cross of the Christ-follower (Christian), thus, belong organically together. God's humanity in Christ can be understood only by human beings who are living in the midst of their everyday reality (instead of those on their way to heaven in the motion of love). Only the sinners and the bad can understand the God who has assumed human beings' sinful nature and who bestows God's own good gifts upon them. Only those who are weak themselves can comprehend God's empowering weakness on the cross. Here we are dealing again with the core of Luther's doctrine of two kinds of love: God is only where God's creating love is, namely, "down" in the humanity, in the "nothingness," and in the "bad" and the "evil."

Christ has united to himself the persons of all sinful human beings. He is, in Luther's words, the greatest sinner (*maximus peccator*), who is immersed (*submersus*) in all sins, and in whom all sins are immersed. Therefore the sin, death, and hell of every human being are in Christ, and Christ, in turn, is in every human being's sin, death, and hell.[7]

Because of the nature of God's love, all God's action in the world has the form and shape of the cross. God works in two ways: God leads human beings into hell and then brings them back again. In other words, God turns human beings into "nothing," making them weak and crazy sinners, but also makes them then "be" and exist again, making them holy, strong, and wise. Luther calls the former action the work of God's left hand, and the latter the work of God's right hand. Luther calls the work of God's left hand God's alien work, and the work of God's right hand Luther names God's proper work. In this context, God's wrath means the same as God's alien work.[8]

It is important to note that the alien and the proper work of God do not take place only in sequence but also, and primarily, "within" each other: God's own proper work is hidden specifically in God's alien work. One of the core ideas of the theology of the cross is that God is always hidden under God's opposite. God's divinity is hidden in God's humanity, heaven is hidden in hell, life is hidden in death, justice and righteousness are hidden in injustice and unrighteousness, power is hidden in weakness, and so forth. God does not work in such a way, for example, as to first make human beings sinners through the work of God's own left hand, and thereafter permanently righteous and just. God's action is constantly and generally hidden under its opposite. Once again, this is a matter of a permanent attribute of God's Love: God's Love does not find but creates that which is lovable in the object of God's Love. Luther says:

> God saves no one but sinners, God instructs no one but the foolish and stupid, God enriches none but paupers, and God makes alive only the dead; not those who merely imagine themselves to be such but those who really are this kind of people and admit it.[9]

In the case of Moses, for instance, the glory of God was veiled as God passed by, and Moses could see only God's backside. Similarly, when God approaches us under the form and in the shape of the cross, we can only see God's visible attributes and the attributes of God's backside, which are the opposite of God's invisible attributes of glory. These visible attributes are connected to God's humanity, and therefore human beings comprehend them only through their own cross and suffering, through their own weakness, foolishness, sin, death, and hell. This is why, according to Luther, life is hidden solely in death, glory in disgrace, holiness in sin, wisdom in foolishness, righteousness and justice in unrighteousness and injustice, power in weakness, and salvation in hell; and, generally speaking, the affirmation of anything good is hidden in its negation. These negations apply both to the cross of Christ and the cross of the human being, because (as stated before) the cross of Christ is identifiable with the cross of human beings.

The purpose of God's alien work is to bring human beings to where God is, that is, not in heaven and its goodness and "what is" but rather below in the world and in its badness and evil and "what is not." This is where human beings actually are, even though they do not admit it to themselves. Therefore, they must be stripped of their false ideas about themselves and of their false ideas about their actual attitudes toward that which is good in relationship with God and fellow human beings. In other words, human beings are shown in a concrete manner that they are not obeying God's law, which, in essence, would demand them to love God and their neighbors. They begin to realize that the commandments of God's law ultimately express what they are lacking in themselves and what they "are not" in themselves.

Thesis 4 in the Heidelberg Disputation reveals how strongly the theology of the cross outlines and determines the content of Luther's view of the law. In order to understand the following passage, we must bear in mind that in God's work of creation, God's law has been written in the heart of every human being. The content of the very core of this law is the demand that human beings love God and their neighbors. Luther says:

> That the works of God are unattractive is clear from what is said in Isa. 53 [:2], "He had no form of comeliness," and in 1 Sam. 2 [:6], "The Lord kills and brings to life; he brings down to Sheol and raises up." This is understood to mean that the Lord humbles and frightens us by means of the law and the sight of our sins so

that we seem in the eyes of human beings, as in our own, as nothing, foolish, and wicked, for we are in truth that. Insofar as we
acknowledge and confess this, there is no form or beauty in us,
but our life is hidden in God (i.e., in the bare confidence in God's
mercy), finding in ourselves nothing but sin, foolishness, death,
and hell, according to that verse of the Apostle in 2 Cor. 6 [:9-
10], "As sorrowful, yet always rejoicing; as dying, and behold we
live." And that it is which Isa. 28 [:21] calls the alien work of God
that God may do God's work (that is, God humbles thoroughly,
making us despair, so that he may exalt us in his mercy, giving
us hope), just as Hab. 3 [:2] states, "In wrath remember mercy."
Such a person therefore is displeased with all one's works; one
sees no beauty, but only one's depravity. Indeed, one also does
those things which appear foolish and disgusting to others.[10]

In order to engender in human beings the correct knowledge
of themselves in relation to God's law, and when beginning to save
them, God leads them into hell. When beginning to make them
holy, God makes human beings sinners, real sinners, not only so in
their own eyes and in other people's eyes. When it comes to natural
Human Love, the theology of the cross is a negative form of theology and God is a negative essence and being; this is so because
God's actions always and repeatedly negate the notion of God
guided by Human Love, according to which God is the sum of all
perfection and is thus a divine God. Admittedly, in agreement with
the theologians of glory, God in Godself is good, righteous, true,
and omnipotent. To human beings, however, God is all this only in
God's humanity, that is, in the oppositeness of the cross and where
human beings are evil, unjust, liars, and powerless. When human
beings, in accordance with their natural love cannot admit this and
thus realize what they really are, God with God's left hand makes
them all that in their concrete realities of life.

It needs to be noted that this work of God's left hand, the purpose of which is to make human beings "nothing" (and this expression, let it be clear, is a synecdoche!), leads precisely to the work of
God's right hand, that is, to allow God to create new things out of
nothingness and emptiness. The ultimate and the primary purpose

of God is not to make human beings into "nothing" and "what is not," sinful, weak, foolish, and damned—in fact, they already are all this. Rather, while in actuality effecting all these things in human beings, God is really wanting them to know, acknowledge, and confess their real, actual weakness, wickedness, and hell—to realize that they are living in separation from God and their neighbors. The distortion of human beings is thus twofold: they are ill but do not recognize their malady; they are lost but do not admit having lost their bearings.

The concepts of God's alien work and God's proper work accurately correspond with Luther's definition of God's Love: God's Love does not find but creates that which is lovable to it. God's Love does not find but creates that which it loves. In other words, God loves that which is deficient and which is evil and bears the marks of foolishness. This means that God loves every human being. Through the work of God's left hand God drives human beings, also externally, so far into the folly and wickedness that they have to finally admit their foolishness and wickedness. This recognition (or admission) is possible, because God's law is, above all, a living law, which is written in every human being's heart and is effective wherever human beings live their everyday lives together. It is effective as a challenge to trust in God, and as the challenge we confront in the faces of our suffering neighbors. Here we are dealing with the very core of the doctrine of two kinds of love:

> All creation teaches that there is no need of a physician except for those who are sick (cf. Matt. 9:12), that no sheep is sought except the one who is lost (Luke 15:4), that no one is freed except the captive, that no one is enriched except the pauper, that no one is made strong except the weak, that no one is exalted except the person who has been humbled, nothing is filled except that which is empty, that nothing is built except that which has been torn down. As the philosophers say: a thing is not brought into form unless there is first a lack of form or a change of previous form; again, a "potential intellect" (*intellectus possibilis*) does not receive a form unless at its origin it has been stripped of all form and is like a tabula rasa.[11]

The philosophical terms used by Luther, the "form" and the "potential intellect," can help us better understand the twofold and paradoxical nature of God's Love. According to the Aristotelian-scholastic scheme of "form and matter," all beings consist of matter (*materia*) and form (*forma*). A piece of stone, for an example, is made of matter that receives its form from a sculptor in accordance with his or her idea. The stone is a potentiality, which receives its form from outside. According to this scheme, the matter is not-anything or "is not," that is, it remains a mere potentiality in relation to the form. The form, then, in relation to the mere potentiality and not-being of the matter, is the reality or being in actuality.

The significance of the "form/matter" schema for understanding God's Love and the theology of the cross has to do with the dialectical tension between "non-being" and "being" or "what is not" and "what is." Just as the pillar of stone could not receive the new form intended by the sculptor without first losing its earlier form, the same way human beings can only receive their new form, and thus their new being, after being stripped from their earlier form. A form can be received only by those missing a form. The paradoxical and twofold nature of God's Love is manifest in this dialectic of taking away the previous form and giving a new form. These events—removing and giving a form—occur simultaneously, just as the work of God's left hand is intimately linked to that of God's right hand.

It seems that Luther is particularly fond of describing the nature and essence of the theology of the cross and with that the understanding of God's Love through the lens of the "matter/form" schema. In his Lectures on Romans he discusses a pivotally important aspect of the theology of the cross, namely, the hiddenness of God's action, which he ties into the "matter/form" schema.

From the point of view of knowing, argues Luther, the works of God and the acts of human beings differ in the sense that an act of a human being can be understood before it takes place. The work of God in human beings, however, can be known only after its completion, and not when this work is still taking place:

Jer. 23:20: "In the latter days you will understand His counsel," which is to say that in the beginning or at first we understand our own counsel, but in the end we understand God's. . . . Just as in the case of an artist who comes upon some material which is suitable and apt for making into a work of art, the suitableness of the material is in a certain sense an unfelt prayer for the form which the artist understands and heeds, as the artist gets ready to make what this material calls for through its suitability, so God comes upon our feeling and thinking, seeing what it is praying for, what it is suitable for, and what it desires; then heeding the request God begins to mold the form which suits God's art and counsel. Then of necessity the form and the model of our thinking is destroyed. Thus we read in Gen. 1:2: "The Spirit of the Lord was moving over the waters, and darkness was upon the face of the deep." Notice that it says, "upon the face of the deep," and not just "upon the deep," for according to appearances it seems to be opposed to us, when the Spirit comes over us and is about to do what we pray.[12]

Because the work of God in human beings is incessant, continuing "from righteousness to righteousness," it remains hidden throughout their lives. Luther says of the Christian: "Again and again one perishes, and yet one is always kept pious."[13]

When working against our affects (our love and thought), that is, against our basic tendency that is part of our notion of good and evil, God looks like a negative essence and being. God seems to be in opposition to all those things which are considered good and true by our unconscious and conscious cry of prayer—which forms our striving toward which is good. God can be possessed and reached only when negating all our affirmatives regarding God. God is a negative goodness, a negative wisdom, and a negative righteousness. In other words, God is the God who is beyond the reach of our intellect, which is guided by our Human Love. God's "being hidden" is so deep that we can say that God is hidden in God's very opposite. Luther states:

For what is good for us is hidden, and that so deeply that it is hidden under its opposite. Thus our life is hidden under death, love for ourselves under hate for ourselves, glory under ignominy, salvation under damnation, our kingship under exile, heaven under hell, wisdom under foolishness, righteousness under sin, power under weakness. And universally our every assertion of anything good is hidden under the denial of it, so that faith may have its place in God, who is a negative essence and goodness and wisdom and righteousness, who cannot be possessed or touched except by the negation of all of our affirmatives.[14]

On the basis of the hiddenness of all God's action we can understand the strong thesis 21 of the Heidelberg Disputation: "A theology of the glory calls evil good and good evil. A theology of the cross calls the thing what it actually is. This is clear: He who does not know Christ does not know God hidden in suffering. Therefore he prefers works to suffering, glory to the cross, strength to weakness, wisdom to folly, and, in general, good to evil." The gospel of the theology of the cross finds its utmost expression especially in these last words of the thesis.

According to Luther, God is not hidden only with respect to God appearing as "nothing" or as a negative essence or a negation in terms of Human Love. God's hiddenness goes even beyond this, actually so far that God even appears as our enemy. This is what hell is about: God as the enemy of human beings, looking like a tyrant who wants hell for human beings. Luther's formulation of this idea in his Psalm interpretation from 1530 is rather shocking:

Outwardly God's grace seems to be nothing but wrath, so deeply it is buried under two thick hides or pelts. God's grace seems to be our opponent and to condemn the world, so that we avoid it like the plague of God's wrath and our own inner feeling about it is not different. Peter says truthfully (2 Peter 1:19) that the Word is like a lamp shining in a dark place. Most certainly it is a dark place! God's faithfulness and truth always must first become a great lie before it becomes truth. The world calls this truth heresy. And we, too, are constantly tempted to believe that God would abandon us and not keep His Word; and in our hearts God begins to become a liar. In short, God cannot be God unless He first becomes a devil. We cannot go to heaven unless we first go to hell. We cannot become God's children until we first become children of the devil. All that God speaks and does the devil has to speak and do first. And our flesh agrees. Therefore it is actually the Spirit who enlightens and teaches us in the Word to believe differently. By the same token the lies of this world cannot become lies without first having become truth. The godless do not go to hell without first having gone to heaven. They do not become the devil's children until they have first been the children of God.[15]

To summarize, the devil does not become and is not a devil without first having been God. He does not become an angel of darkness unless he has first been an angel of light (2 Cor. 11:14). For what the devil speaks and does must first have been said and done by God. This the world believes and would have us believe. Therefore these are deep words, and a profound understanding is required to grasp that God's grace and truth, or God's love and faithfulness, rule over us and prevail. But it is comforting to him who can grasp it, if he is sure that all is God's grace and truth, even when it seems to be the opposite, and if he can then say in spiritual defiance: "I know well that God's Word must first become a great lie, even in myself, before it can become truth. I also know that the devil's word must first become the delicate truth of God before it can become a lie. I must grant the devil his hour of godliness and ascribe devilhood to our God. But this is not the whole story. The last word is: 'His faithfulness and truth endure forever.'"[16]

When investigating in more detail God's actions as opposite to Human Love and to the form this love desires, we need to pay attention to the essentially important point that the oppositeness is not just something imagined or something existing merely in thought. Nor does God regard God and human beings as opposite to one another only on the level of thought; the oppositeness is real. Just as it is real that God saves only those who are sinners, crazy and without understanding, those who are poor, weak, dead, and lost. This being the case, the theologian of glory abandons this kind of God.

God's action stands in real opposition to what is desired by Human Love of the human beings, who, nevertheless, are the matter of God's work. The suitability of the matter with the form, that is, human beings' reaching toward "what is" and what has a good form, is simultaneously human beings' natural love toward their own good. The theologians of glory, says Luther, are at the same time both God to themselves and the neighbor to themselves; they relate to both God and their neighbor as if to themselves. Natural human beings use (*uti*) both God and their fellow human beings for their own purposes, enjoying (*frui*) themselves as their ultimate end. Consequently, God must remove this defective form, that is, to make it into "nothing" or "what is not," in order to be able to create something new. God's action in this scenario, thus, seems to rather hurt human beings than to listen to and meet their desire, which is signified in their very existence.

> Hence it results that when we pray to God for something, whatever these things may be, and God hears our prayers and begins to give us what we wish, God gives in such a way that contravenes all of our conceptions, that is, our ideas. After our prayers God may seem to us to have more offended and to do less after we have asked than before. And God does all this because it is the nature of God first to destroy and tear down whatever is in us before giving us God's good things, as the Scripture says: "The Lord makes poor and makes rich, He brings down to hell and raises up" (1 Sam. 2:7, 6).[17]

In light of the concept of the hidden God described above, we can understand the ultimate purpose of Luther's criticism of "metaphysics" as he knew it. In metaphysics, in Luther's view, the attributes of God are explored on the basis of the theology of glory. In other words, God's attributes are observed directly as they appear in their divine glory but not in their hiddenness in their opposites. Metaphysics, then, cannot address or observe the hidden God, but the obvious God, the kind of God pictured by human beings in accordance with their own love, Human Love. Luther's criticism of metaphysics (and of the theology of glory) can be formulated as follows: the metaphysicians, or metaphysical theologians, regard God and God's action as a direct extension of the kind of inclination toward good that is signified by the mere existence of human beings. The form of the God of metaphysicians is a direct extension of the form already existing in human beings, in accordance of which God does not need to remove the previous, old form of the subject matter when giving them a new form. Ultimately, says Luther, metaphysicians do not understand that God loves that which is nothing in order to bring it into being, and that God's left hand therefore must first empty the objects of God's Love. The God of the metaphysicians is a solely right-handed God. Luther points out very clearly the fundamental fallacy of metaphysics:

> But do we not preach again and again that God's power, wisdom, goodness, righteousness, and mercy are great and marvelous without understanding them? For we understand things metaphysically, that is, according to the way we understand them, namely, as things that are apparent and not hidden, although He has hidden His power under nothing but weakness, His wisdom under foolishness, His goodness under severity, His righteousness under sins, and His mercy under wrath. Hence they do not understand the power of God when they see infirmity, etc. Thus Ps. 81:7: "I answered you in the secret place of thunder." Note the expression "the secret place," which means: when the thunder of wrath hid the sweetness of mercy, that is, when He hears us by doing the opposite of our expectations. We ask for salvation, and He, to save us, increases our damnation and hides His answer under this kind of thunder. This is symbolized in Exod. 5:5ff., where, when He was about to set the people free, He aroused Pharaoh the more strongly against them, so that He seemed to be less desirous of saving them.[18]

Luther's doctrine of the theology of glory and the theology of the cross can be considered a variation on the theme of two kinds of love. God's way of creation is to create out of nothing, which means "oppositeness": it means that God brings down the mighty and exalts the lowly, and that God kills in order to bring back life.

In order to understand Luther's theology of the cross correctly, we must keep in mind that many of its pivotal expressions (such as "destruction" and "annihilation") are synecdoches, which Luther likes to use (as mentioned above). Accordingly, Luther talks about God's acts of "striking" and "destroying" and killing in a following manner:

> Synecdoche, to be sure, is a most sweet and necessary figure of speech and a symbol of God's love and mercy, for sometimes when He is said to strike and destroy, one is not to understand that He strikes all or completely annihilates, for He touches the whole when He touches a part.[19]

Furthermore, to comprehend correctly Luther's theology of glory and theology of the cross, we must bear in mind that by distinguishing between these two theologies, Luther is ultimately only restating Jesus' controversial teaching about who would enter the kingdom of God and who not: according to Jesus, tax collectors and prostitutes would enter the kingdom of God before the scribes and Pharisees. Luther elaborates on Jesus' teaching and states that those who "wish to be justified and made alive" through works and the law, will

> fall further short of righteousness and life than do tax collectors, sinners and harlots. These latter cannot rest on confidence in their own works, which are such that they cannot trust that they will obtain grace and the forgiveness of sins on their account. . . . Therefore such people are more fortunate than the self-righteous in this respect; for they lack trust in their own works, which, even if it does not completely destroy faith in Christ, nevertheless hinders it very greatly. On the other hand, the self-righteous, who refrain from sins outwardly and seem to live blameless and religious lives, cannot avoid a presumption of confidence and righteousness, which cannot coexist with faith in Christ. Therefore

they are less fortunate than tax collectors and harlots, who do not offer their good works to a wrathful God in exchange for eternal life, as the self-righteous do, since they have none to offer, but beg that their sins be forgiven them for the sake of Christ.[20]

Luther's theology of the cross deals with this same oppositeness between human righteousness and the righteousness of faith. In addition, and in distinction, the theology of the cross has the idea of oppositeness elaborated in the general context of the basics of Christian faith: that is, in light of and in relation to the doctrine of creation, God's providence in human beings' daily lives, the person of Christ, and so forth. The theology of the cross is thus one particular expression for the understanding and idea of God, who is pure giving love and who does not seek good but unites good with that which is otherwise deficient and evil or bad.

4. Two Kinds of Love and the Worth of Creation

Quite appropriately we can consider Luther's concept of faith as the core of his Reformation program. It is also best to explore the content of this concept from his idea of two kinds of love.

When understanding human beings' relationship with God on the basis of Human Love, religious life is seen as a movement from the world toward the supreme good and the highest object of love, namely, God. The realization of this kind of motion of love, understood here according to the Aristotelian model, is, ultimately, human activity or a human act or work (*ergon*) (as demonstrated above in chapter 2). The human being is saved in the motion and act of love, even if not for the sake of the motion or act.

When the relationship with God is understood within the framework of God's Love, however, the active agent and subject is God, not the human being. Because God is pure and outward-flowing love, God's essence and being is thus an incessant act of giving. God works in such a way that God does not seek "what is" and that which is good, but rather God unites existence or being and good to that which has no existence or being of its own, or which is evil and bad. The existence and being and the good which God gives to human beings include everything that is precious in the created world. Above all, however, they include God, that is, God's merciful essence with all God's divine riches, which are righteousness, holiness, power, joy, life, and so forth. The "site" or the "organ" within and through which God unites God's goodness to human beings, and within and through which human beings receive God's love, is faith. In Luther's theology, faith is the fundamental concept for understanding God-human relationship, whereas in those interpretations that are based on the notion of Human Love the key concept is "appetitive love." Thus, the core of Luther's Reformation program finds its expression in the following statement: "But where they [the scholastics] speak of love, we speak of faith."[1] This does not mean that love for God would not still be important for Luther, but that he understands this love being born or emerging in faith and as its consequence; it cannot be understood from the model of appetitive love (see below, chapter 7, "Love for God" in Luther's theology). The difference between the two notions of faith, one based on the idea of receiving faith and the other on the notion of appetitive love, becomes manifest already when considering how human beings should be relating to their God the creator, that is, in assessing what would constitute a right attitude and right ways of relating to the creation and all its goodness and preciousness. Those interpretations of Christian faith that understand human beings' relationship with God through the concept of appetitive love inevitably tend to have a more or less negative attitude toward the world. In these interpretations, love for God always stands fundamentally in competition with any kind of love for any transitory good in God's creation, this so in spite of any attempts to safeguard against this tendency. Thus, the intensity of Christians' love for God can be seen as inversely proportional to the intensity of their love for something that belongs to the created world.

The basic competitive relationship between love for God and love for the precious things in God's creation is evident, for example, in Augustine's notion of love, which fundamentally influenced Catholic theology before Luther's time. Admittedly, Augustine tried to combine the ideas of God's Love and Human Love in their wholeness, but the notion of appetitive love still occupied quite an important place in his thinking. According to Augustine, there are two kinds of love: the love that uses its object as a means to an end, called *uti* love, and the love that enjoys its object, called *frui* love. In the enjoying kind of love, *frui* love, the object of love is loved as an end in itself, whereas in the love that uses its object, *uti* love, something is loved as a means to reach the goal of enjoyment, *frui*. At the core of Christian teaching of faith there is an expectation that human beings abandon the wrong order of love and discover the right order of love. Augustine thinks that only God may be loved with the enjoying *frui* love—that is, for the sake of the lovability of the object that is being loved—whereas all creatures are to be loved only with *uti* love, for the sake of the lover itself. In spite of Augustine's teaching that true love for God is bestowed upon human beings by grace alone, the basic mode of human beings' relationship with God is nevertheless *frui*, which Augustine understands very much in accordance with the pattern of appetitive love. At this point, Augustine's thought contains some permanent problems that have to do with, first, human beings' relationship with the precious aspects of the creation and, second, their love of other human beings as a goal in itself. What exactly does it mean that a human being loves either a precious thing in the created world or another human being with *uti* love, that is, as a means to love God? Indeed, attention has been paid to the fact that the notion of unselfish and giving love for one's neighbor is hardly given sufficient space in Augustine's thought. Furthermore, it has been noted that Augustine hardly discusses the love between a man and a woman, and that as far as this particular question is concerned, he has left an empty space in the history of the concept of love in the Western world.[2]

When interpreted on the basis of Human Love, the relationship with God follows the general rules of movement, according to Thomas Aquinas's teaching: appetitive love has God as its object and involves first a detachment from the "prior position," before moving toward a new end and the final stage of rest or joy in the union with the ultimate goal. This interpretation of the human beings' relationship with God with the appetitive love is manifest, for instance, in *The Imitation of Christ* by Thomas à Kempis. In the following, when introducing this work from the viewpoint of Luther, and thus from a perspective actually alien to *The Imitation of Christ* itself, the intent is certainly not to disparage the value of this masterpiece among the spiritual classics. In fact, Luther himself, in spite of his criticism, speaks highly of Thomas à Kempis. Nor is it the intention here to make an issue of the "opposite" stances represented by the Lutheran and the Catholic traditions, especially given the fact that after Luther's time, both traditions have applied the idea of appetitive love in their interpretation of God-human relationship. In any case, Thomas à Kempis's thinking as a whole is clearly shaped by the idea of appetitive Human Love, even if at the very heart of his thinking we can find also something that resonates with Luther's thought. The theme of God's love is expressed using a strong language of Human Love, resulting in a complex amalgamation that is difficult to analyze. The theology of Thomas à Kempis demonstrates how human beings' appetitive love for God and the human beings' (expected) abandonment of the precious things of the creation, or world, belong inseparably together. Because this point is crucial for Luther's doctrine of the two kinds of love, a more detailed look at the thought of Thomas à Kempis is in order.

First, using Augustine's concepts of *uti* and *frui* love, Thomas à Kempis teaches that human beings need, above all, the right order of love. God alone is to be enjoyed, whereas creatures are only to be used. Thomas à Kempis says:

> Be patient, my soul; await the fulfilment of God's promise, and you shall enjoy the abundance of His goodness in Heaven. But if you hanker inordinately after the good things of this life, you will lose those of heaven and eternity. Therefore make right use of this world's goods, but long only for those that are eternal. This world's good things can never satisfy you, for you are not created for the enjoyment of these alone.[3]

Human beings must detach themselves from where they are and move toward the highest and real good, the only good that lasts. This happens through an activity or an act, by which individuals prepare themselves for grace, and which leads them to the abandonment of the world and detachment from it. Thomas à Kempis says:

> My son, My grace is precious, and may not be mingled with worldly concerns and pleasures. Therefore, if you wish to receive it, you must remove every obstacle to grace. Seek out a place apart, and love the solitary life. Do not engage in conversation with men, but instead pour forth devout prayer to God, that you may preserve a humble mind and a clean conscience. Count the whole world as nothing, and place attendance on God before all outward things.

For you cannot attend on Me, and at the same time take pleasure in worldly things. Remain detached from acquaintances and friends and independent of this world's consolations.[4]

In Luther's theology of the cross, it is God who makes human beings empty and "what is not," or "nothing" in the concrete situations of their lives, and human beings are objects of this activity, not active agents in it. Thomas à Kempis, in turn, teaches that it is human beings' active abandonment of the world and their refusal to love that which is attractive in the world or creation that makes them into a vacuum into which the grace of God can flow. Even the slightest affection for worldly goods hinders them from attaining the highest good, the highest object of love. Thomas à Kempis expresses this as follows:

> If you would perfectly destroy self and empty yourself of love of creatures, I would infuse all My grace into you. But while your interest is in creatures, the vision of the Creator is hidden from you. Learn, then, for love of the Creator, to overcome self in everything, and you shall come to the knowledge of God. But so long as anything, however small, occupies too much of your love and regard, it injures the soul and holds you back from attaining the highest Good.[5]

Almost word for word, Thomas à Kempis gives voice to what Luther calls the theology of glory: The Creator has nothing in common with creatures. The theology of glory looks to the highest good when loving instead of looking "down" in faith into a "human" God. Thomas à Kempis says:

> Rapt in spirit, a man must rise above all created things, and perfectly forsaking himself, see clearly that nothing in creation can compare with the Creator. But unless a man is freed from dependence on creatures, he cannot turn freely to the things of God.[6]

The more we define love for God and love for the world or creation as exclusive opposites, the more we end up describing human beings' relationship with God through concepts and images characteristic of the active and appetitive Human Love—in this case, love between a man and a woman. Thomas à Kempis first describes the efforts of love and its movement toward the loved one:

> Nothing is sweeter than love, nothing stronger, nothing higher, nothing wider, nothing more pleasant, nothing fuller or better in heaven or earth; for love is born of God, and can rest only in God, above all created things. . . . Love flies, runs, and leaps for joy; it is free and unrestrained. Love gives all for all, resting in One who is highest above all things, from whom every good flows and proceeds. Love does not regard the gifts, but turns to the Giver of all good gifts. Love knows no limits, but ardently transcends all bounds. Love feels no burden, takes no account of toil, attempts things beyond its strength; love sees nothing as impossible, for it feels able to achieve all things. Love therefore does great things; it is strange and effective; while he who lacks love faints and fails.[7]

Having first described the detachment of love from the world and then the active movement of love toward the loved one, Thomas à Kempis finally portrays the end of this motion: the rest or joy in the loved one. Love surges upward like a living flame, until it is dissolved and plunges itself into that love which is God in God's divinity:

> Love is watchful, and while resting, never sleeps; weary, it is never exhausted; imprisoned, it is never in bonds; alarmed, it is never afraid; like a living flame and a burning torch, it surges upward and surely surmounts every obstacle. Whoever loves God knows well the sound of His voice. A loud cry in the ears of God is that burning love of the soul which exclaims, "My God and my love, You are all mine, and I am Yours."

> [A Prayer] Deepen Your love in me, O Lord, that I may learn in my inmost heart how sweet it is to love, to be dissolved, and to plunge myself into Your love. Let Your love possess and raise me

above myself, with a fervour and wonder beyond imagination. Let me sing the song of love. Let me follow You, my Beloved, into the heights. Let my soul spend itself in Your praise, rejoicing for love. Let me love You more than myself, and myself only for Your own sake. Let me love all men who truly love You, as the law of love commands, which shines out from You.[8]

Thomas à Kempis's conception of Christian faith—even with its discernible emphasis on God's Love—is an illustrative interpretation of a Christian faith that is based on the idea of appetitive human love and that has love for God and love for the precious things of the created world standing in basic competition and opposition with each other. This kind of principal conflict between the two is not found in Luther's notion of the human beings' relationship with God—a notion determined by a particular concept of God's Love and by a particular concept of faith as the "organ" receiving this love. When the starting point is the notion that "to be God is not to receive but to give," then God is not, primarily, the recipient or the end of appetitive human love. A true relationship with God is not constituted by an active, appetitive love, but by faith that receives. In God's "giving" goodness, God bestows upon human beings God's gift of "pure" love for God and also "pure" love for their neighbors—"pure" meaning freedom from both fear of punishment and hope for reward.

In Luther's view of Christian faith, already the creation of the world is in accordance with God's way of granting and giving: it is characteristic of God to create something out of nothing. The good that God bestows upon human beings in creation is really a good gift of God, which human beings can in faith receive as God's goodness.

> I hold and believe that I am God's creature; that is, that he has given me and constantly sustains my body, soul, and life, my members great and small, all my senses, my reason and understanding.[9]

Even existence, "being," in itself is a gift from God. Luther makes a poignant observation for the theologians of glory to consider:

What would happen if God took away the air human beings breathe, even for the duration of one single prayer!

Sin is not primarily about attachment to something good that God has created, but rather quite the contrary: While it should be the case that human beings' "hearts will be warmed and kindled with gratitude to God and a desire to use all these blessings to his [God's] glory and praise," this does not happen, and that is sin.[10] This does not mean that human beings should be grabbing and seizing the good gifts of God for themselves, but rather that they should thank God for these gifts and pass on to their neighbors both these gifts and the joy they engender.

It is especially important to notice that Luther may have been the first theologian to link God and the material world, God and "matter," so closely to each other. On this point we can recognize, once again, Luther's theology of the cross and the related idea of "oppositeness." Human Love tends to spiritualize God and place God in heaven, beyond the material world, while, in fact, God is present precisely in those places that look the least like God in the eyes of human beings, namely, in matter and in material reality. God's Word that created (that is, the Word with which God created and creates) once made the material world come into being, and all God's action within creation is still bound to matter. Providence, incarnation, the written word and the Word that echoes as a living voice, the sacraments, and the church as a community of people who support and sustain each other are all part of the concrete and material world, within which God is hidden. Furthermore, Christians' works of love are also directed to other human beings and their physical and spiritual needs, rather than being oriented upward toward a "spiritual" God in the movement of the appetitive love. God is always a material and human God—both in Christ and in Christians, who are Christs to their neighbors.

God and material reality belong together; that is evident in Luther's fresh attitude toward sexuality, among other things. In the words of Heiko A. Oberman:

> Luther's association of "higher" and "lower" powers in man shows that something decisively new was underway. The surprising element—one still highly offensive in the sixteenth century—was

the assertion that sexual drives were a divine force or even God's vital presence. Luther found the scriptural basis for his view in a verse from the Book of Genesis. The passage became so important to him that he made repeated attempts to translate it into good German, ultimately deciding for the version: "Es ist nicht gut, dass der Mensch allein sei. Ich will ihm ein Gehülfen, die um ihn sei, machen" (Gen. 2.18), which corresponds precisely to the King James Version: "It is not good that the man should be alone; I will make him a help mate for him." Luther's exegesis of the text, informed by his thoughts on sexuality and marriage, is truly epoch-making. "This is the Word of God, by virtue of which . . . the passionate, natural inclination toward woman is created and maintained. It may not be prevented by vow and law. For it is God's Word and work." God's power is not confined to marriage; it is already present in the sexual instinct. Marriage is simply the right way to use it, the genuinely spiritual, divinely ordained status to live one's sexuality. Because the Devil hates God's life-giving power, he hates marriage with the same intensity and seeks to hinder the peace of God and to decrease the fruits of the earth.[11]

Indeed, Luther teaches that abstention from marriage does not give anybody a special "holier than others" status; besides, such abstention is possible only with God's special and clear calling and for the purpose of a distinct labor of service. Marriage, in turn, belongs to everyone and is a noble and divine estate. Luther insists that whoever is ashamed of marriage is also ashamed of being and being called human, and tries to improve on what God has made.[12]

It is as impossible for a man to be without a woman, or for a woman to be without a man, as it would be for anyone to be without food, drink, sleep, or other natural necessities of life.

Now if someone wants to stop this [i.e., sexuality] and not permit what nature wants and must do, what is he doing but preventing nature from being nature, fire from burning, water from being wet, and man from either drinking, eating, or sleeping?[13]

Luther's view of sexuality and marriage is only one part of the new conception of reality that emerges when Christian faith is interpreted on the basis of God's Love. The entire earthly, created reality gains a new significance and worth when it is viewed as a God-given gift and a mission to be received in faith. When the basic concept defining the relationship with God is faith as the recipient of God's good gifts, the works of the active motion of love no longer need to turn in the direction of God, because God, in all God's essence, is already present in faith as love; instead, they turn in the direction of neighbors, in order to share that which is good with those who are in need. Christians, thus, do not need to suffer from the kind of abstinence that comes from the practice of self-chosen deeds and does not benefit their neighbors at all. The true suffering and the true cross are not engendered by self-chosen works but by participation in the need and want seen in the suffering neighbor's face. This gives the free Christian the crucial position to consider how best to help the neighbors in the midst of their concrete life situations. All this imparts a deeply spiritual nature and character to human beings' actions in their families and different callings and functions in society. How impressive the calling or action is does not matter. For instance, when a scribe sits in his chamber, he does good to others and loves his community; therefore, his room is a dwelling place of the Spirit of God. In the same way, the Holy Spirit rejoices when the husband helps his wife and washes their child's dirty diapers, and so forth.

This breakthrough view of the earthly reality as a deeply spiritual reality manifests itself especially clearly in his notion of the law of God. Unlike the interpretations of Christian faith that are based on the idea of Human Love, in Luther's understanding God's law is not an eternal order (*ordo*) of love that determines the earthly and divine reality.[14] Rather, the law demands that human beings, in their concrete lives and different life situations, have faith in God and love their neighbors. In other words, the law demands that human beings believe in the goodness of God, receive that goodness, and share it with their neighbors. Because of the reality of sin, God also works through God's law and providence so that human beings either recognize their incapability to believe in God in and by themselves and to love their neighbors—or that they become increasingly blind to what they are missing. Therefore, God cannot be the object of faith merely insofar as God is the creator and the giver of the Law (that is, as the God of the first article of the Creed), but, above all, faith is directed toward God who has been given to human beings in Christ. In Christ, God bestows upon human beings not only the good gifts of the created world but also God's own divine essence. In Christ, God begins to restore and return the paradise where God is in the hearts of human beings, and human beings are in one another's hearts—the paradise where God is the dwelling place for human beings and human beings are the dwelling place for one another. In other words, God is beginning to recreate a rule of love.

5. Faith and God's Creative Love for "What Is Not" and for "Evil"

In Luther's theology, God's Love finds its most powerful expression in the person of Christ. In Christ, God has not only manifested a merciful attitude toward human beings but also has given Godself entirely to human beings. Faith is essentially about receiving this merciful and self-giving God's Love, which human beings encounter in Christ.

To grasp how Luther understands the way in which faith receives this merciful self-giving of God, we have to examine his theology of the word, or Word.

Luther's theology of the word/Word is based on the distinction between the internal and the external word. The internal word is the awareness or thought in the human mind through which human beings experience their own will, thoughts, and emotions. In a way, this awareness is human beings' speech to themselves. The internal word reveals to human beings what they are in themselves. In order to express themselves to others, to persons who are "outside" of them, the human beings' only possibility is to let the internal word become incarnate in a material sign: in a spoken or written word, or a facial expression or a gesture. Thus, in order to be understood, the internal word must clothe itself with a material, external word.

The external word has a twofold influence. On the one hand, it is only through the external word that a human being can know and have access to the internal word of another human being, that is, to what the other individual is and experiences. On the other hand, the material, external sign also hinders one from understanding the inner reality of another human being. That is, one's internal word is never immediately or directly within the reach of another individual, but always only through an external, material sign. Because there is no direct route from the internal word to the world outside (the only route being the external word), the material sign always also covers and hides the internal word. Thus, a human being hears the speech of another individual but cannot understand (or "get") the message it bears; in other words, the external word is not transformed in the listener into an inner reality that would correspond with the inner reality of the speaker.

According to Luther, what has been said here of the human beings' internal word and external word also applies to God and God's Word, with some essential differences. In God, too, there is the internal Word, the Logos, which is Godself: God's wisdom, thought, power, life, righteousness, goodness, and so forth. Furthermore, the internal Word of God must also take upon itself the form of a material sign so that human beings could grasp and understand it. The internal Word of God must clothe itself with flesh, that is, with the external Word of God. Christ is this incarnate Word of God. Everything that Christ is, says, and does is God's external Word to human beings.[1]

There is one point, however, where Christ as the Word of God differs decisively from what the words of a human being are for another human being. In the case of the human word, the person of the speaker is involved only to a certain extent, whereas in the case of the "Christ Word," the person of God is present totally and fully and in an absolutely real manner. Luther says of the human word:

> However, also the human word shows something of this, because it is in the human word [menschlich wort] that the human heart is known. It is a commonplace to say, "I know [literally: I have] his heart," or, "I know [literally: I have] his mind," even though one actually only knows [has] the word of the other. This can be said because the mind of the heart follows the word, and is known through the word, as if it were in the word. Experience has taught the pagans, too, so that they say: "A human being speaks what he is," and, "Speech is the reflection of the heart."[2]

What applies only partially to the human word, however, applies totally to God's Word: God's essence or being is totally present in the Word that God speaks.

> God's word is so much like God that the whole of divinity is in it, and whoever has the word, has the whole of divinity. But for this reason, this metaphor [that God's word is like the human word] also proves wanting. That is, the human word does not bring with it the essence or nature of the heart, but makes the heart present only on the level of meaning, or merely as a sign, just as an image made of wood or gold does not bring with it the human essence that it signifies. But in the case of God, the word brings with it not only the sign or image, but the whole essence, and the word is as full of God as is the one whose image or word it is.[3]

Luther's theology of the Word can be understood only in the context of his theology of the cross. The inner, "metaphysical" Word of God cannot be known by human reason, which is led by human love; instead, this knowledge is always broken and led into "nothing" by the oppositeness of the cross. Even in God's Word of revelation, God is hidden. First, the divine Word has hidden itself in the opposite constituted by a material sign, namely, human flesh. Second, and even more profoundly, the Word is hidden in the sense that instead of assuming neutral and pure human nature, it has taken upon itself real and concrete human nature. The Word of God has clothed and united itself with its ultimate opposite, that is, the weakness, folly, sin, suffering, death, and hell of the human being. The Word of God has the form of the cross. Therefore, only those who are of the same form as God's Word can grasp and know it. We can understand God's speech only when we "see" it through the cross and suffering, that is, in our own sin, weakness, foolishness, suffering, death, and hell. The Word of God can be encountered only where God's Love is: where it is creating new in the midst of nothingness and evil and that "which is not." Human reason and Human Love, each of which turn toward "what is" and that which is good, ignore and pass by the incarnate Word (as do those who are righteous and wise and happy with their knowledge and whatever else they possess).[4]

Even though God's word of revelation is hidden under its opposite so deeply that it looks like nothing, as something that "is not," it nevertheless is God Godself. Out of pure goodness and love for human beings, God—that is, God's Word—is clothed with human burden and need and has taken it all upon Godself. God's attitude toward our need, sin, death, and hell is as if these were God's own. In accordance with the golden rule, the Word plunges itself into the depths of humanity, weakness, and foolishness; in so doing, God gives Godself and God's attributes (divine power, wisdom, righteousness, joy, etc.) to human beings. An exchange of properties occurs between us and the Word. In Christ, God has overcome our weakness by becoming weak, thus uniting power with weakness. God has conquered our sin by becoming sin [in Godself] and by becoming cursed [in Godself], thus uniting that which is righteous and blessed to that which is sinful and cursed. God has shown that God is greater than death and doom by dying and becoming doomed [in Godself], thus uniting life with death and mercy with doom. God has entirely and fully stepped in the place of the human being. The Word has become flesh so that the flesh might become Word.[5]

All that Christ does manifests the way God acts, in its extreme manifestation: God's Love turns its direction to "where it does not find good which it may enjoy, but where it may confer good upon the bad and the needy." "The love of God [God's Love] does not find, but creates, that which is pleasing to it." Even though, according to Luther, the work of Christ is not "of one kind but of all kinds" (e.g., incarnation, atonement, redemption), goodness and love nevertheless characterize everything that Christ does.[6] Faith receives this merciful and self-giving God's Love; that is, it receives the Word that has become incarnate in Christ.

According to Luther, participation in Christ takes place through the word of the gospel. The gospel is the message of Christ. Christ is the external Word of God, in whom God's internal Word is hidden. Furthermore, the Word of God, that is, God in Godself, is also hidden in the spoken or written Word of Christ, that is, in the gospel. Here again we come across the notion of oppositeness, which is an essential part of Luther's theology of the cross. From the point of view of human reason, which is directed by human love, God is hidden in the material sign of the word (that is, in the letter, or the voice, which can be heard "here and now") and in the visible word (that is, the sacraments). In the word of the gospel, therefore, God looks like "nothing" or "what is not." Only faith can receive this Word, because faith is the kind of knowledge that sees nothing. Only in this darkness and cloud of faith does God wish to be present. How exactly God is present in it, human reason cannot comprehend. This is about the idea of oppositeness that is inherent in the theology of the cross. Only that which has no form can receive form. Only the kind of knowledge or knowing that knows nothing, the kind of knowledge or knowing that has been stripped of the desire to have or possess the form of that which is good and "what is," can through the Holy Spirit be the seat of God's presence and thus a sanctuary in a human being. "The flesh sees nothing there and comes to this conclusion: out of nothing, nothing comes into being. Nevertheless, through the word of consolation we see in this 'nothing' everything that is to come."[7] Luther compares faith with the "holy of holies" prepared by Moses in the tabernacle, the place of darkness. Precisely this darkness is the dwelling place of God.[8]

Human beings can receive the word of the gospel only through faith—faith being the locus of this reception. In the darkness and "nothingness" of the faith itself, then, the Word of God, Christ, is present with all God's divine attributes: righteousness, wisdom, power, holiness, life, joy, love, and so forth. In faith, the "Christ Word" unites with human beings, so that they would unite with the "Christ Word." In this way, also in faith the Word itself takes on a particular likeness of human beings, so that human beings might take on a likeness of the Word. Wisdom becomes folly, so that folly might become wisdom, power becomes weakness, so that weakness might become power, and so forth. The Word does not change into a human (that is, it does not become a human being), however, but it becomes the likeness of human beings. In the same way, the human beings are not transformed into being the Word, but into the likeness of the Word.[9]

In faith, "God's life" fights against the powers of destruction present in human beings. Just as fire burns iron, so the life of God renews the believers and makes us alive. The righteousness of God drives away human unrighteousness, God's holiness destroys our sin, God's joy makes our sadness and depression disappear, God's love makes our hatred and selfishness vanish, and God's immortality drives death away. It must be noted again, however, that in accordance with the theology of the cross, the real and efficacious presence of Christ is to be experienced in "what is not," in "nothingness," and in the darkness of the oppositeness. God dwells only in those who feel that in themselves they are furthest from God and nearest to Satan. Such a human being is a "lovely residence, castle, hall, and paradise where God lives on earth."[10]

The Word of the gospel unifies God and sinners. Luther says about the significance of this word:

> [Let us then consider it certain and firmly established that] the soul can do without anything except the Word of God and that where the Word of God is missing there is no help at all for the soul. If it has the Word of God it is rich and lacks nothing since it is the Word of life, truth, light, peace, righteousness, salvation, joy, liberty, wisdom, power, grace, glory, and of every incalculable blessing.[11]

The central content of Luther's Reformation is at stake here:

> The Word of God cannot be received and cherished by any works whatever but only by faith. Therefore it is clear that, as the soul needs only the Word of God for its life and righteousness, so it is justified by faith alone and not any works.[12]

There is a passage in the larger version of Luther's *Lectures on Galatians* in which he pulls together in a unified vision, first, the doctrine of the two kinds of love; second, the notion of the real presence of Christ in the darkness of faith; and, third, the doctrine of justification, which is the central doctrine of the Reformation. Most of the central themes in Luther's theology interpreted here can be recognized in this text:

Where they speak of love, we speak of faith. . . . But if it is true faith, it is a sure trust and firm acceptance in the heart. It takes hold of Christ in such a way that Christ is the object of faith, or rather not the object but, so to speak, the One who is present in the faith itself. Thus faith is a sort of knowledge or darkness that nothing can see. Yet the Christ of whom faith takes hold is sitting in this darkness as God sat in the midst of darkness on Sinai and in the temple. Therefore our "formal righteousness" is not a love that informs faith; but it is faith itself, a cloud in our hearts, that is, trust in a thing we do not see, in Christ, who is present although he is utmost hidden from our sight. Therefore faith justifies because it takes hold of and possesses this treasure, the present Christ. But how He is present—this is beyond our thought; for there is darkness, as I have said. Where the confidence of the heart is present, therefore, there Christ is present, in that very cloud and faith. This is the formal righteousness on account of which a man [human being] is justified; it is not on account of love, as the sophists say. In short, just as the sophists say that love forms and trains faith, so we say that it is Christ who forms and fulfills faith or who is the form of faith. Therefore the Christ who is grasped by faith and who lives in the heart is the true Christian righteousness, on account of which God counts us righteous and grants us eternal life. Here there is no work of the Law, no love; but there is an entirely different kind of righteousness, a new world above and beyond the Law. For Christ or faith is neither the Law nor the work of the Law.[13]

To summarize, in Luther's view the true relationship with God does not emerge in the movement or "work" of the appetitive, desiring Human Love toward God but when human beings receive God's Love in the gospel through faith. According to Luther, God raises from the dead only those who are dead, just as Christ raised Lazarus from the dead with his word. Luther says:

Before God, you must not do any other work than to believe that Christ does His works for you and sets them before God. And, in order to keep your faith pure, do nothing; just be quiet and let Him do what is good; receive His work, and let Him practice His love on you. You must be blind, lame, deaf, dead, leprous, and poor, or otherwise you will become incensed at Christ. The gospel does not lie to you when it says that Christ can be seen only among these kinds of people, that is, among those who are in need, and that He does His good deeds only among them.[14]

Even if Luther emphasizes that human beings are entirely in the receiving end in their relationship with God, his position can be fully understood only when taking into consideration what he says about God's Love as the unifying power that unites God and human beings. It is fair to say that Luther is a representative of a particular doctrine of divinization, to use a concept from the early church. In agreement with the common heritage of Christian churches, Luther teaches that the Word became flesh, so that the flesh might become Word. This applies primarily to Christ, but it also applies to Christians in the sense that Christ is truly present in their faith. Thus, the presence of Christ means a particular kind of divinization of Christians. Their essence does change or become the Word, but Luther nevertheless thinks that, because of the union of the Word and the Christian, it is possible to say that Christians in themselves are the Word itself. Luther explains:

We, who are flesh, do not become Word in the sense that our substance would change into the substance of the Word, but in the sense that we assume the Word and unite it to ourselves through faith. Because of this union, it is said not only that we have the Word but that we even are the Word.[15]

Because the Word is Christ, it can also be said that the Christian "is Christ." This said, Luther's view of Christians as Christs is interpreted entirely wrongly if understood on the basis of Human Love. But from the starting point that "to be God" signifies giving rather than receiving, then "to be Christ" means being somebody who gives also. God gives Godself to that "what is not" and that which is bad or evil, and this is also the task of Christians in their relationship with their neighbors. This is why Luther calls Christians

"Christ(s)," and this is what Luther means with the expression of being "Christ to one's neighbors." Luther says, for example, "I will therefore give myself as a Christ to my neighbor, just as Christ offered himself to me."[16]

Thus, when the idea of divinization and the notion of God as the Giver are combined, we can see that Luther's view of Christians as Christs to their neighbors is rooted in the very fundamentals of his theology. The nature of this view of divinization is also expressed in the following passage:

> Hence, as our heavenly Father has in Christ freely come to our aid, we also ought freely to help our neighbor . . . and each one should become as it were a Christ to the other that we may be Christs to one another and Christ may be the same in all.[17]

Moreover, Luther even says that Christians are called Christians precisely because Christ dwells in them and they are thus Christs to one another:

> We are altogether ignorant . . . of our own name and do not know why we are Christians or bear the name of Christians. Surely we are named after Christ, not because he is absent from us, but because he dwells in us, that is, because we believe in him and are Christs one to another and do to our neighbors as Christ does to us.[18]

In Luther's theology, the "passivity" of faith—that is, receiving from God that which is good—and the "activity" of love, that is, giving to one's neighbor that which is good—belong together; the glue between the two is in the idea of the presence of Christ and divinization. The summary of Christian faith and life can be drawn from this:

> We discover daily so many new works and doctrines that we finally end up knowing nothing of the true and good life. That is, the whole of Christian doctrine, all works, and life in its entirety

are included briefly, clearly and overflowingly in two points, which are faith and love. Through them, a human being is placed between God and one's neighbors as an instrument that receives [gifts] from above and then passes [them] on below, thus becoming a vessel or channel through which the spring of divine goods flows into other people without interruption. This is what those who truly have the form of God are like; they receive from God everything God has, in Christ; and through good works they, in turn, prove to be as if they were gods to others. This is the realization of Ps. 81 (82:6): "I say, 'You are gods, children of the Most High, all of you.'" We are children of God through faith, which makes us heirs to all divine goods. In turn, we are gods through love, which makes us do good to our neighbors; namely, the divine nature is nothing but beneficence and, as St. Paul says here, friendship and love for human beings which pours its good gifts daily upon all creatures, as we can see.[19]

6. Christians as "Christs" to Their Neighbors

Luther's concept of the two kinds of love provides an access to his notion of neighborly love: The relationship of human beings with God is not about the appetitive movement toward God, as would be the case with Human Love ordinarily, but rather about human beings receiving God's Love, all of which takes place in faith. Christians' works of love, then, are freed to serve other people. Luther expresses this idea in a phrase he often repeats: "Do to your neighbor what Christ has done to you."

> Except for faith, we must direct all our works to our neighbors. That is, God does not demand of us any works intended to serve God Godself, but solely faith through Christ. This is sufficient to God, and therefore we honor God as the One who is gracious, merciful, wise, good, truthful, etc. Therefore, think only to do to your neighbor what Christ has done to you, and let all your works and your whole life serve your neighbor. Find out where the poor, the sick, and all kinds of needy people are, and help them. Put your life in practice there; let those who need you enjoy you, as much as you can, and do this with your body, property and honor.[1]

As mentioned above, the law of God demands from us faith and love. The fulfillment of the law is bestowed upon Christians in Christ; that is, in him Christians rediscover both God and their own neighbors.

In order to understand correctly the idea of Christ as the one who fulfills the law in human beings' relationship with God, it must be noted that love encompasses all the commandments of the second table of the law, that is, the commandments concerning human relationships.

> Love is the head and source of all virtues—all in all, the virtue of all virtues. Love feeds you, quenches your thirst, clothes you, comforts you; love prays for you, sets you free, helps you and saves you. What should one say? Inwardly and outwardly, love gives itself, its body and life, its property and honor and all its strength to the need of the neighbor, to the neighbor's advantage, be that friend or foe; it holds back nothing through which it may help him. Therefore, no virtue can be compared to love. Moreover, love will not be described or named through any single particular work, as can be done in the case of the other, partial virtues, such as chastity, mercy, patience, lenience, etc. Love does it all . . . so that St. Paul says that all commandments are summed up in these words, "Love your neighbor as yourself."[2]

Because love is the source and root of all commandments, it both establishes and annihilates all commandments:

> This commandment of love is a short commandment and a long commandment; it is one single commandment and many commandments; it is no commandment at all and it is all commandments. That is, it is short and one in itself, and as far as the intellect is concerned, one grasps it quickly. But it is long and many from the point of view of practice, because it encompasses all commandments, being the master commandment. Furthermore, it is no commandment at all if one thinks about works, because there is no one single particular work related to it. However, it is all commandments, because the works of all commandments are, and must be, works of this commandment. Thus, the commandment of love annihilates all commandments and yet establishes them all.[3]

All laws, both mundane and ecclesiastical, have the same goal, which is love:

So many books and doctrines have been written to teach people how to live their lives that they can be neither counted nor numbered. And yet there is still no end to the writing of books and laws, as we can see regarding spiritual and temporal justice. . . . All this would be bearable if . . . those laws and doctrines were drawn from the main law and rule and standard of love, and treated in accordance with it. This is what the Holy Scripture does; it also gives many kinds of laws, but gathers and places them all within the framework of love, subjecting them all to love. Wherever love is involved, there all these laws have to yield, ceasing to be laws and ceasing to be valid any longer.[4]

According to Luther, the need of the neighbors is the criterion for neighborly love. This principle is expressed in the golden rule, the shortest version of which reads: "Love your neighbor as yourself." This rule means that all human beings are in principle able to know what others need; all that is needed is that they place themselves in the position of others and deem from there what they would wish for themselves in each situation. Luther says:

It is a brief statement, expressed beautifully and forcefully: "You shall love your neighbor as yourself." No one can find a better, surer, or more available pattern than himself; nor can there be a nobler or more profound attitude of the mind than love; nor is there a more excellent object than one's neighbor. Therefore the pattern, the attitude, and the object are all superb. Thus if you want to know how the neighbor is to be loved and want to have an outstanding pattern of this, consider carefully how you love yourself. In need or in danger you would certainly want desperately to be loved and assisted with all the counsels, resources, and powers not only of all men but of all creation. And so you do not need any book to instruct and admonish you how you should love your neighbor, for you have the loveliest and best of books about all laws right in your own heart. You do not need any professor to tell you about this matter; merely consult your own heart, and it will give you abundant instruction that you should love your neighbor as you love yourself. What is more, love is the highest virtue.

It is ready to be of service not only with its tongue, its hands, its money, and its abilities, but with its body and its very life.[5]

It must be noted that Luther's interpretation of the golden rule can be understood correctly only in the context of the pure love of God and as an expression of this love without self-interest. That is, the golden rule challenges us human beings to love our neighbors for their sake, not for the sake of any good or advantage we might gain from them.

> For through this expression, "as yourself," every pretense of love is excluded. Therefore he who loves his neighbor on account of his money, honor, knowledge, favor, power, comfort, and does not love the same person if he is poor, lowly, unlearned, hostile, dependent, unpleasant, clearly has a hypocritical love, not a love for him himself, but a love for his neighbor's goods for his own benefit, and thus he does not love him "as himself," for indeed, he does love himself, even if he is a pauper, or a fool, or a plain nothing. For who is so useless that he hates himself? But no one is such a nothing that he does not love himself and does not love others in the same way. Therefore this is the hardest commandment of all, if we really think about it.[6]

Luther's idea that no one is such a "nothing" that he or she would not wish to be loved shows clearly how the reformer interprets the golden rule on the basis of God's Love, which orients toward "what is not" and that which is evil.

It is characteristic of Luther's concept of neighborly love that he does not accept the loving person's good intention as such as the criterion for the moral goodness of an act. The golden rule places such a criterion outside the loving person in the needs and good of the other person. As an example of the unsuitability of the lover's good intention as the criterion of love, Luther mentions the way rich people use their money:

> [R]ich men supply the priests with treasures for the building of a church or a memorial. But if they would put themselves in

the position of the poor and ask themselves whether they would want it donated not to themselves but rather to the churches, they would easily learn from themselves what they ought to do.[7]

According to Luther, the internal good intention and the external good work belong together:

> And so St. Paul rejects the dreams of the scholastics who speak of love in such a way as to separate the external deed and the internal favorable intention from each other. They say that love is an internal favorable intention which loves the neighbor when it gives the neighbor what is inwardly good. . . . Pay no attention to such words. That is, you can see here that for St. Paul love is not a mere favorable intention but also a good and favorable deed.[8]

In accordance with the concept of God's Love, Christian love means for Luther that Christians help other human beings through concrete works, according to their neighbors' needs. This kind of love thus follows the principle of God's Love, as it does not pursue good for itself but gives and shares goodness with others:

> It [the commandment of love] does not say: "You shall love the rich, the mighty, the learned, the holy. . . ." On the contrary, there are no acts of favoritism in this kind of love. It is the wrong, fleshly and worldly love that shows partiality; it loves only as long as loving brings with it advantage and hope, and where there is no more advantage or hope, there love is at an end, too. But this commandment demands of us an unforced love for everyone, regardless of who they are and whether they are friends or foes. Namely, love seeks neither advantage nor good things, but gives and does them to others. Therefore love is at its most active and mighty where it is love for the poor, needy, evil, sinful, foolish, sick and the enemy. There it has its hands full of bearing, suffering, carrying, serving and doing good.[9]

The nature of Christian love as divine love that turns toward "what is not" and that which is bad or evil manifests itself particularly clearly in Luther's concept of love for sinners. In Luther's theology, love for sinners is a pivotal theme (the same cannot be said always about the later forms of Lutheranism). Luther often says that while it is a great thing to help the neighbors externally, it is even greater to love the sinners and to cover their sins with righteousness.

> If we let our property become the servant of the other person, we perform a very great external work of love. The greatest work, however, is that I give away my righteousness and let it serve my sinful neighbor. That is, when I serve and help the neighbor externally with property my love remains alone, but to extend righteousness to one's neighbor is to do something great; in order to do so, I must be at peace and I must love . . . I must love my neighbor so much that I search for the neighbor and become like the shepherd who searches for his sheep, or the woman who searches for her lost coin.
>
> Therefore, we want to speak here of this noble work of love: that a pious man defends a sinner with his own righteousness, and a pious woman defends the worst harlot with her own honor. The world and reason do not do such things. That is, where only reason prevails, and where there are only pious and upright people, such things cannot be done. Instead, these people want to show their righteousness only by their ability to turn up their noses at sinners.[10]

Furthermore, Luther states the following about the love for sinners:

> These are the true Christian works: that the Christian falls and plunges into the mud where the sinner is, and is immersed in it as deeply as the sinner is; and that the Christian takes the sinner's sins upon oneself, and rises up again with the sinner, acting as if those sins were one's own.[11]

In his programmatic 1520 treatise *The Freedom of a Christian* (*De libertate christiana/Von der Freiheit eines Christenmenschen*), Luther says on the same theme:

See, according to this rule the good things we have from God should flow from one to the other and be common to all, so that everyone should "put on" his neighbor and so conduct himself toward him as if he himself were in the other's place. From Christ the good things have flowed and are flowing into us. He has so "put on" us and acted for us as if he had been what we are. From us they flow on to those who have need of them so that I should lay before God my faith and my righteousness that they may cover and intercede for the sins of my neighbor which I take upon myself and so labor and serve in them as if they were my very own. That is what Christ did for us. This is true love and the genuine rule of a Christian life.[12]

The example set by Christ for loving sinners means, according to Luther, that Christian life in its entirety is about bearing the load of other people's sin. This notion is also important for Luther's concept of the church: by and large, Christians associate only with sinners.

With one single word, St. Paul condemns the essence and rule of all hypocritical holiness. That is, it is true of the hypocritical that they cannot associate with those who are sinful and infirm. Everything must take place in accordance with their rigid law. Thus, what takes place is just chase and hunt; there is no mercy but only punishment, reproach, judgment, reprimand and rage.

As for Christians, however, it is true of them that there are a great deal of sinners and infirm people among them; indeed, they associate with them and not with the holy. Therefore, Christians reject no one but carry everyone in their arms and take care of these people so compassionately as if they were suffering from their infirmities themselves; they pray for them, and teach, urge and encourage them, doing everything they possibly can in order to help them. This is what true Christianity is like; this is what God has done to us in Christ, and still does.[13]

Because Christians associate only with those who are sinners and deficient and needy, Luther says, the church can be nothing else but a hospital for those who are irrecoverably ill. The sum of the gospel is that the kingdom of Christ is a continuous condition of caring for one another. For this reason, bishops and priests were to act as if their diocese was a hospital and as if they were dealing with only the sick.

> This is the sum of the gospel: the Kingdom of Christ is a kingdom of mercy and grace. It is nothing but bearing and more bearing: Christ bears our infirmities and diseases; He takes our sins upon himself and is patient with us when we go astray, bearing us all the time on His shoulders and never getting tired of bearing us. Those who are preachers in this Kingdom shall comfort consciences, associate amiably with people, feed them with the gospel, bear the weak, heal the sick . . . and give everyone what they need.
>
> This is what the ministry of a true bishop and preacher is like. They are not supposed to use violence, as do our bishops who beat people, put them in the stocks and cry: "There, there, who does not want to, he must!" No; a bishop or preacher shall act like a person who cares for the sick, treats them carefully, shares good words with them, speaks with them pleasantly and amiably and takes care of them in every possible way. This is how also a bishop or priest is supposed to act; he is supposed to think that his diocese or parish is a hospital for those who are irrecoverably ill, a hospital with many sick people with various diseases.[14]

A fundamental theme in Luther's ecclesiology is his concept of Christians as Christs to one another. Just as Christ has given himself to Christians in the bread and wine of the Holy Communion, in the same way Christians are one bread and one drink in Christ. In this way, Christians are the bread and the drink to satisfy one another's hunger and thirst.

> It is true of us, too, that we all become one cake and eat each other. You know that when bread is being made, all the grains are crushed and ground into flour, and each grain becomes the flour of another grain, that is, the grains are mixed with each other. In

a sackful of flour you can see how the grains have been crushed against each other so that every grain has become the flour of another, and none of them has retained its shape. Each grain gives its flour to another grain, losing its own body, so that the bodies of these many grains become the body of one single loaf of bread. The same thing happens in the making of wine: each grape mixes its juice with the juice of the other grape; each of them loses its shape, and they become one juice. This is what is to happen also with us; I make myself common to all of you and serve you, so that you use [*geniessen*; actually "enjoy"] me for the purpose for which you need me. So I am your food, just as you eat [*geniessen*] bread when you are hungry, for it to help your body and hungry stomach and give you strength. Therefore, when I help and serve you in all your need, I am also your bread. Moreover, if you are also a Christ[ian], then you, in turn, do the same thing to me: you serve me with everything you have, so that it all works for my good, and I can use [*geniessen*] it like food or drink. If I am a sinner, and you, by the grace of God, are godly, then you come to me and share your godliness with me, and you pray for me, and you appear before God on my behalf and act toward me as if I were you. You "eat" my sin with your godliness, just as Christ has done to us; and if you eat me, then I, in turn, eat you.[15]

Luther thinks that all human activities are in principle meant to be in the service of love. The sharing of good takes place through the proclamation of the gospel and the feeding of the poor, just as through other activities in the family, society, and church. It is true, though, that under God's earthly rule or in the temporal judicial systems love is forced love: the judicial system protects the weak from the violence of the stronger with the sword of the governing authority. Even the forced love is one of God's ways of loving and conveying good to human beings. Also the judicial system and the sword borne by the temporal authority are servants of love. Human beings' activities in church and society thereby spring out of love and nurture, and they protect the life God has created.

7. Love for God

The structure of Luther's thinking of Christian faith as a whole can best be understood from the perspective of two kinds of love (as discussed in the previous chapters), namely, Human Love and God's Love. "Where they [the scholastics] speak of love, we speak of faith"; this proposition of Luther concerning the essence of human beings' relationship with God can be taken as the focal theme of his program of reformation. In other words, instead of speaking of Human Love, which pursues God as the highest good, Luther wants to speak of faith: faith means receiving God's Love that is oriented toward that "what is not" or is evil and deficient. Luther does not see the relationship with God as a relationship based on active and appetitive love, or as a relationship marked by works (*iustitia activa, iustitia operum*), but rather as a relationship of receiving and based on "passive" faith (*iustitia passiva, iustitia fidei*).

This basic definition concerning the relation between God's Love and Human Love brings forth two questions to ponder. First, what is the role of Christians' love for God in Luther's overall understanding of Christian faith? To be sure, throughout the reformer's works he does speak about the believer's love for God. Second, Luther often says that Christians' love for God must be stronger than their love for any creature. This being the case, does Luther's Christian worldview necessarily entail a fundamentally negative attitude toward the world—the kind of negativity that inevitably follows when the relationship with God is understood as a relationship based on the appetitive love that functions in accordance with Human Love, and the kind of negativity that causes a permanent, principal, and unsolvable conflict between love for God as the highest good and love for the created beings as less valuable goods?[1] The distinction between Human Love and God's Love is a premise central to Luther's theology as a whole, but on this particular issue of Christians' love for God, does the distinction become relativized? The two questions become one fundamental question: is it possible to understand Christians' love for God as an organic part of Luther's theology of "two kinds of love"?

The question about Christians' love for God and its place in Luther's theology has stirred surprisingly insufficient discussion. For example, the scholarly debate on Anders Nygren's thesis concerning the place of *eros* and *agape* love in Luther's theology has not resulted in even a single monograph dealing with Luther's understanding of the love for God that finds its realization in faith.[2]

First, it is obvious that, in the theology of Luther, Christians' love for God is based on God's love, which turns to and is oriented toward that "what is not" and that which is evil or bad and deficient. God's love is the foundation for Christians' love for God. In *The Magnificat*, for example, Luther says this absolutely unambiguously, immediately after describing the movement of Human Love toward the heights, on the one hand, and the movement of God's Love into the depths, on the other:

> Therefore to God alone belongs that sort of seeing that looks into the depths with their need and misery, and is near to all that are in the depths; as St. Peter says (1 Peter 5:5): "God opposes the proud but gives grace to the humble." And this is the source of human beings' love and praise of God. For no one can praise God without first loving God. No one can love God unless God makes Godself known to the human being in the most lovable and intimate fashion. And God can make Godself known only through those works of God that God reveals in us, and that we feel and experience within ourselves. But where there is this experience, namely, that God is a God who looks into the depths and helps only the poor, despised, afflicted, miserable, forsaken, and those who are nothing, there a hearty love for God is born. The heart overflows with gladness and goes leaping and dancing for the great pleasure it has found in God.[3]

In this passage Luther argues that God's Love is the basis for Christians' love for God. He repeats the conclusion by saying, for instance, that God's Love, which turns toward the depths, is the reason for human beings' love and praise of God: "Thus God's work and God' eyes are in the depths, but human being's are only in the height. This is the reason for Mary's canticle."[4]

Christians' love for God emerges from their getting to know God's Love: that God looks to the depths and turns God's eyes to "what is not." Luther says, "In short, this verse teaches us to know God aright, because it shows us that God regards the lowly and despised. For one knows God aright who knows that God regards the lowly. . . . From such knowledge flows love and trust in God, by which we yield ourselves to God and gladly obey God.[5]

In faith, Luther teaches, human beings are united through the Word with God; because God is love, human beings become also unified with the divine love in that very faith.[6] When Christ lives in Christians through faith, love begins to "live" in them as well, as Luther expresses it in the Heidelberg Disputation.[7] It is important to notice that the love that Christians have received in faith is directed or oriented not only toward other human beings, but also toward God. This love for God that "lives" in faith is not a human accomplishment, not a "work of a man or a woman," but a work of God. Christians are objects of this work of God and under the influence of this work of God and they experience this as a "joyful passion" (suffering). Luther says:

> My life and all my senses float in the love and praise of God and in lofty pleasures, so that I am no longer mistress of myself; I am exalted, more than I exalt myself, to praise the Lord.
>
> This is the experience of all those who are saturated with the divine sweetness and Spirit: they cannot find words to utter what they feel. For to praise the Lord with gladness is not a work of man; it is rather a joyful suffering [passion] and the work of God alone. It cannot be taught in words but must be learned in one's own experience.[8]

Because Christians, in faith, participate in God's own love, which, in turn, effects in human beings love for God and their neighbor, this effective love also has the attributes of God's Love: it is without self-interest and does not seek its own. Christians begin to love both God and other human beings with a "pure" love that is without self-interest. It is important to notice, then, that Christians also love God with a pure love that does not seek its own. (This thought has gone rather unnoticed in Luther research.)

According to Luther, love for God is pure when human beings love and praise God only because of God's goodness, not because of the good gifts they receive from God. The opposite are the "impure lovers" or "parasites" (*nieszling*), who wish to enjoy and use what they love, rather than loving the mere goodness of God without self-interest; they are concerned only about themselves and are constantly measuring how much God shows God's goodness to them in tangible and experienced ways. Luther says:

> Thereby she [Mary] teaches us to love and praise God for Godself alone, and in the right order, and not selfishly to seek anything at God's hands. This is done when one praises God because God is good, regards only God's bare goodness, and finds his joy and pleasure in that alone. That is a lofty, pure, and tender mode of loving and praising God and well becomes this Virgin's high and tender spirit. But the impure and perverted lovers, who are nothing else than parasites and who seek their own advantage in God, neither love nor praise God's bare goodness, but have an eye to themselves and consider only how good God is to them.[9]

The impure love for God lasts only as long as it brings with it good things and benefits for the one who loves. Where God does not allow the impure lover to have this experience and benefit, there also love for God dies; impure lovers do not want to be poor and without merit themselves. Therefore, when God withdraws God's own goodness, leaving human beings in their misery and poverty, also the love and praise of God come to an end. When human beings love God with self-interest, they cannot praise the divine goodness hidden in those works of God that seem opposite to God.

For this kind of impure love, the gift is dearer than the Giver. Luther describes these "parasites" whose love for God is impure:

> But just as soon as God hides God's face and withdraws the rays of God's goodness, leaving them bare and in misery, their love and praise are at an end. They are unable to love and praise the bare, unfelt goodness that is hidden in God. By this they prove that their spirit did not rejoice in God, their Savior, and that they had no true love and praise for God's bare goodness. They delighted in their salvation much more than in their Savior, in the gift more than in the Giver, in the creature rather than in the Creator. For they are not able to preserve an even mind in plenty and in want, in wealth and in poverty; as St. Paul says (Phil. 4:12): "I know how to abound and how to suffer want."[10]

In Luther's theology, as described above, the pure love for God is not separate from faith. On the contrary, faith is part of the actual definition of pure love for God. That is, pure love for God clings to God's love, even though God's love is hidden behind the curtain of oppositeness and can be discerned by faith alone, that is, by the "knowledge that knows nothing." Pure faith includes precisely the pure love for God. As an example, Luther lifts up Mary, who praises God:

> It is indeed a spirit that exults only in faith and rejoices not in the good things of God that she felt, but only in God, whom she did not feel and who is her salvation, known by her in faith alone. Such are the truly lowly, naked, hungry, and God-fearing spirits.[11]

This passage reveals how closely Luther's view of Christians' pure love for God is connected with his general and full concept of faith, and thus with his doctrine of the two kinds of love and the theology of the cross. This connection manifests itself even more clearly in the following brief discussion of the relation between the doctrine of justification and pure love for God.

If we are to analyze the relation between justifying faith and Christians' love for God, we must remind ourselves of the fact that

God's law ultimately demands from human beings two things: "You shall love the Lord your God with all your heart, and with all your soul, and with all your strength, and with all your mind; and your neighbor as yourself" (Luke 10:27). According to Luther, this love for God demanded by the double commandment of the law, defines the pure love for God in the following way: "purity" cannot be only a negative kind of freedom that comes from seeking one's own benefit, but also a positive kind of freedom that comes as an "overwhelming" fullness in one's mind and essence or being—precisely the kind of love Luther describes above with the example of Mary.

In faith, human beings receive Christ as a gift, and Christ is (to use Luther's expressions) the fulfillment of the law and the end of all its commandments. In other words, the spontaneous, free, and unforced love for God and neighbors is given to human beings in faith. Faith, however, is not a law, nor is it as such the fulfillment of the law. Rather, it "acquires," "brings with itself" or "gives" love, which, in turn, is the fulfillment of the law. Luther says:

> Even though faith itself does not fulfill the law, it nonetheless has that by which the law is fulfilled. That is, faith acquires the Spirit and love, and the law is fulfilled with these. On the other hand, even though love does not justify, it gives evidence of what we are justified by, namely, faith. In sum, when St. Paul himself says that love is the fulfillment of the law [Rom. 13:10], it is as if he were saying that being the fulfillment of the law, on the one hand, and acquiring or giving it, on the other, are two different things. Thus, love fulfills the law by being itself the fulfillment of the law, whereas faith fulfills the law by bringing with itself that with which the law is fulfilled. Namely, faith loves and is effective, as is said in Gal. 5 [:6]: ". . . faith working through love." Water fills the vessel, and so does the waiter (faith): the water with itself, the waiter with the water. This is what the sophists mean when they speak of "effective et formaliter implore" [the effective, actual, and real fulfillment of the law].[12]

This text expresses accurately what Luther means when he says that the spontaneous, joyful love for God is not a human accomplishment but a work of God in the human being. In faith and in its darkness, in "what is not," the Spirit of God makes the Word, Christ, to be present in human beings. Furthermore, God fills human beings with Christ and with all Christ's attributes, that is, with God. Luther says:

> We are filled in all the ways in which God fills a person. We are filled with God, and God pours into us all God's gifts and grace and fills us with the Spirit, who makes us courageous. God enlightens us with God's light, God's life lives in us, God's beatitude makes us blessed, and God's love causes love to arise in us.[13]

Justifying faith belongs inseparably together with the pure love that is based solely on the goodness of God. Faith, that is, human beings' trust in God and in God's love hidden in its opposite—the trust that "resides" in the "holy of holies" and so in its "darkness"— is what makes human beings loving; this happens solely because of God's goodness.

Thus, the fact that justifying faith and pure love for God belong together can be analyzed positively by studying the relation between love and justifying faith. It can also be analyzed negatively, by showing the affinity between impure love and the "righteousness of works" that Luther criticized. That is, in Luther's view the righteousness of works is based on self-seeking love. First, when human beings try to be justified and blessed through "works," they seek in God their own good and salvation; their love for God is then not based on the gracious goodness of God alone. They try to "purchase" blessedness, that is, their own good, by their works. Second, when human beings pursue salvation through their works, their works of love are not performed only for the sake of the good and advantage of their neighbor; rather, the intended end of these works is the lover's own good, his or her salvation. Thus, those who pursue justification through works love both God and other human beings impurely and with distortion. Pure and "true" love, in turn, arises only from the confidence of the heart in the goodness and mercy of God.

Luther understands both the love for God and the love for neighbor as something that arise from faith, that is, from the confidence of the heart. This understanding enables Luther to present the entire Christian life with its respective relations to God and neighbors through the image of love between a man and a woman. What he emphasizes there, though, is the confidence that prevails in this kind of love relationship, rather than its appetitive or desiring nature. Luther uses the image of the relationship between a man and a woman, for example, in his *Treatise on Good Works*:

> When a husband and wife really love one another, have pleasure in each other, and thoroughly believe in their love, who teaches them how they are to behave one to another, what they are to do or not do, say or not to say; what they are to think? Confidence alone teaches them all this, and even more than is necessary. For such a man there is no distinction in works. He does the great and the important as gladly as the small and the unimportant, and vice versa. Moreover, he does them all in a glad, peaceful, and confident heart, and is an absolutely willing companion to the woman. But where there is any doubt, he searches within himself for the best thing to do; then a distinction of works arises by which he imagines he may win favor. And yet he goes about it with a heavy heart and great disinclination. He is like a prisoner, more than half in despair, and often makes a fool of himself. Thus a Christian man who lives in this confidence toward God knows all things, can do all things, ventures everything that needs to be done, and does everything gladly and willingly, not that he may gather merits and good works, but because it is a pleasure for him to please God in doing these things. He simply serves God with no thought of reward, content that his service pleases God. On the other hand, he who is not at one with God, or is in a state of doubt, worries and starts looking about for ways and means to do enough and to influence God with his many good works . . . and yet finds no peace. He does all this with great effort and with a doubting and unwilling heart, so that the Scriptures rightly call such works in Hebrew *aven amal*, that is, labor and sorrow. And even then they are not good works and are in vain. . . . Of these it is written in Wisdom [of Solomon] 5 [:6], "We have wearied ourselves in the wrong way and have followed a hard and bitter

road; but God's way we have not acknowledged and the sun of righteousness has not risen upon us."[14]

While describing the relationships of Christians with God and their neighbors as love relationships, however, Luther does not give up his fundamental theology of faith: love is realized in such a confidence of the heart, that is, faith, which is based on God's goodness alone, in other words, on "God's Love."

Christians' love for God can be understood as an organic part of Luther's theology of the two kinds of love. What remains to be clarified is the idea often repeated by Luther: that Christians' love for God must be stronger than their love for any creature. Does the reformer fall here into the same pitfall of the fundamental denial of the created world's preciousness that he elsewhere so sharply criticizes as a characteristic trait of the religiosity based on Human Love?

To outline and simplify, the answer to this question is as follows: When Luther contrasts love for God with the love for the created good, he does not deny the preciousness and worth of the good creation. All the goods given in creation and redemption, such as money, property, body, spouse, children, friends, wisdom, knowledge, spiritual gifts, and so forth, really are good gifts of God. They are, however, indeed good gifts of God that are to be received as given by God. In one way or another, it may happen to human beings that some goods to which they truly are entitled are taken away from them, or they just do not have them. In this case, they must not cling to these goods and rights in such a way that their clinging to these things or their attempt to obtain them or take them back again causes even greater damage to themselves and others. They must recognize and acknowledge that their goods and rights really are good and right; otherwise they would deny God's word. This truth, however, does not entitle them to get angry at God and be bitter toward God if God decides to take any of the gifts away from them for a while or for good. In a situation like this, God tries and tempts human beings in order to see whether they love the gift more than the giver, that is, whether they love God with pure love. The loss of good must not be a reason for anyone to "rage and storm and take it again by force." In other words, to recognize the good and right is one thing, to obtain or win it is another. Human beings are supposed to recognize and acknowledge their good and their right, but if they do not manage to obtain them, they are to leave them to God and be trusting and calm, in the state of "*Gelassenheit*" ("du solt der selben gelassen stehen").[15] This is the context for the commandment to love God more than created beings. Christians must trust in the sheer goodness of God and not lose this trust in anger and bitterness if God should mask any of God's goodness in the withdrawal of gifts.

I quote here a passage where Luther says with particular clarity how loving God more than creatures does not imply the denial of the preciousness of the creation or the created beings:

> In this way the truth is not denied, for the truth declares they are good things and God's creatures. But the same truth declares also and teaches that you should let such good things go, be ready at all times to do without them, if God so wills it, and cleave to God alone. The truth, by saying they are good, does not compel you to take the good things back again, nor to say they are not good; but it does compel you to regard them with equanimity and to confess that they are good and not evil.
>
> In the same manner we must treat the right and the manifold good things of reason or wisdom. Who can doubt that right is a good thing and a gift of God? God's Word itself says right is good, and no one should admit that his good and righteous cause is unrighteous or evil, but should sooner die for it and let go of everything that is not God. To do otherwise would be to deny God and God'sWord, for God says right is good and not evil. But if such right is snatched from you or suppressed, would you cry out, storm and rage, and slay the whole world? Some do this; they cry to heaven, work all manner of mischief, ruin land and people, and fill the world with war and bloodshed. How do you know whether or not it is God's will that you keep such a gift and right? It belongs to God, who can take it from you today or tomorrow, outwardly or inwardly, by friend or foe, just as God wills. God tries you to see whether you will dispense with your

right for the sake of God's will, be in the wrong and suffer wrong, endure shame for God, and cleave to God alone. (If you) fear God and think: "Lord, it is yours; I will not keep it unless I know you will me to have it. Let go what will: only be my God...."[16]

The passages where Luther contrasts love for God with love for creatures seem to find their explanation in the context described above. No fundamental conflict between the love for the created good and the love for God can be found in any of these passages. On this point, too, Luther's understanding of Christians' love for God is to be understood as part of his full theological vision and the structure of his whole theology.

Afterword: Finnish Luther Research since 1979

by Juhani Forsberg

Martin Luther has had a central role in the theological history and church life of Finland since the time of the Reformation, identified with the leadership of Mikael Agricola (coinciding with the Swedish Reformation during the reign of King Gustaf Vasa in 1527, under whose rule Finland was at the time). This relationship first happened through the translation of Luther's works into the new written language of Finnish and later through ongoing academic research on Luther's works. Until our time, Luther's works have been translated into Finnish and distributed in different venues. For instance, in 2000, a modern translation of Luther's Small Catechism was distributed to about two million Finnish households. The roots of the modern and distinctively Finnish research on Luther can be dated to the end of the nineteenth century, a tradition that has continued with strength ever since.

This afterword focuses on the latest stage of the Finnish Luther research, namely, since 1979,[1] highlighting some of the most important academic monographs published to date. The purpose here is to introduce works that are—at least for now—available only in Finnish and thus not accessible to an international audience (apart from individual lectures and specific translations). Given the space limitations, articles or collections, even if noteworthy, are left out,[2] as is the vast amount of Luther literature produced for a broader audience and for educational purposes (and often heavily based on scholarly work on Luther). Nor is there space here to address the international scholarly responses to the Finnish Luther research.[3] Needless to say, the selected works that are lifted up are introduced as neutrally and objectively as possible, even if the author of this article himself comes from the circle of the Finnish Luther research.

Tuomo Mannermaa's Work in Historical Perspective

At the turn of the year 1973–1974, Bangkok, Thailand, hosted a conference of the Commission on World Mission and Evangelism of the World Council of Churches with the general theme "Salvation Today." In this conference, the issue of salvation was addressed exclusively and one-sidedly as a social-ethical phenomenon, which evoked sharp criticism from the representatives of the Russian Orthodox Church and independently from the Evangelical Lutheran Church of Finland and its representation. The theme of salvation was addressed again in a bilateral dialogue in 1974, during which further critique of the one-sidedness of the Bangkok conference became formulated. A further opportunity to discuss the theme of salvation more thoroughly came at the next round of dialogues in Kiev in 1977.

Those preparing for the conference on behalf of the Evangelical Lutheran Church of Finland posed a fundamental question: What did the Lutheran Confessions and especially Martin Luther teach about salvation? What is the most genuine and central teaching we could bring to the table with our Orthodox discussion partners? In Kiev, Professor Tuomo Mannermaa (b. 1937), then professor of Ecumenical Theology, held a presentation on the topic of the relationship and connections between the Lutheran doctrine of justification and the patristic-orthodox doctrine of divinization (*theosis*). On the basis of a thorough and fresh reading of Luther's own texts, Mannermaa came to conclude that Luther's doctrine of justification did not stand in "diametrical opposition" to the orthodox doctrine of divinization after all, a position that ran counter to the arguments of some of the most important Protestant teachers of the nineteenth and early twentieth centuries (Albrecht Ritschl and Adolf Harnack, in particular). Between the two doctrines, Mannermaa acknowledged, definite differences remained in both terminology and content, but, he argued, there were also clear similarities in content and terminology between the two. This meant that the two traditions had connecting points to the degree that they could not simply be separated, even if they could not be considered identical either. Later Mannermaa would develop his findings in a more detailed and carefully documented research with a title "In ipsa fide Christus adest" ("Christ is present and active in faith itself," a citation from Luther's large commentary on Galatians).[4] With this study Mannermaa turned to Luther with a special perspective in mind. Let it be acknowledged here that the dialogue with the Orthodox Church going on at the time admittedly played a role as a catalyst in this new research, and its outcomes were to be seen in the works of Mannermaa and later also in the works of his students. In spite of this, however, it is not self-evident or certain that the discussions with the Orthodox partners should be given a defining significance in this new interpretation of Luther's theology. As Risto Saarinen has concluded, Finnish Luther research takes as its primary task that of interpreting the historical Luther, whether or not the picture of Luther that emerges has any ecumenical relevance.[5]

The main findings of Mannermaa's research have to do with two central and interconnected themes: (1) the doctrine of justification and (2) the connection between faith and love. The most important finding in Mannermaa's research is that Luther's doctrine of justification sets him clearly apart from Melanchthon and the authors of the Formula of Concord, and that the heart of Luther's teaching was to be found in his two central formulations: "in ipsa fide Christus adest" (Christ is present and active in faith itself) and "fides est creatrix divinitatis" (faith is the creator of divinity)—naturally not "in sua substantia" but "in us."

Mannermaa's reading demonstrated a basic difference between Luther's understanding of the doctrine of justification and other approaches applied by Melanchthon and the Formula of Concord: in the confessional writings, the forensic and judicial (in foro coeli; imputare) perspective was in the forefront, whereas the indwelling of Christ "in us" was understood only as the result or the consequence of imputative righteousness. For understanding the Lutheran Confessions' teaching of justification in full, it is important to realize that the Formula of Concord, which develops no specific distinct teaching of justification of its own or "in extenso" but mostly argues against "wrong" teachings, explicitly lifts up Luther's Galatians commentary as the most authoritative source on justification, the same text where the two above-mentioned key phrases can be found.

After Luther's student Andreas Osiander had criticized Melanchthon's teaching, and justifiably so—without getting Luther's teaching necessarily right himself either and becoming rejected by his fellow reformers—the centrality of the expression of the indwelling of Christ in faith in the Lutheran confessional teaching became doubtful and dubious and nearly forgotten. This happened in spite of the fact that the idea was very clear and central in Luther's own teaching.

In the present book, *Two Kinds of Love: Martin Luther's Religious World*, Mannermaa demonstrates first how Luther's interpretation of love was different from that of the scholastic theology. According to the late medieval theory, love would form a "unitive power" (*vis unitiva*) and orient itself toward the good and worthy, whereas according to Luther, God's love directed itself toward "nothing" and toward that "which was not." Love would produce something that was to be good and beautiful out of its object, which was "nothing" in itself. This statement was made in Luther's Heidelberg Disputation and could be seen in different variations in Luther's writings; this statement would form the basis for Luther's theology of love, as proved further in Mannermaa's ensuing examination.

Mannermaa came to the conclusion that Luther's view on love had become understood too one-dimensionally: as love sent by God through faith, further expressed in the believer as love of the neighbor. He concluded that the long-prevailing concept from Anders Nygren that set *eros* and *agape* loves as opposites to each other—a premise he uses to interpret the entire history of theology, including Luther's—does actually not work with Luther's theology at all. With Nygren's perspective, Luther's position came to be interpreted too one-sidedly, only as love that came from God through faith and which then was lived further in neighborly love. But we must seek to understand Luther's idea of human love for God in its late medieval context and in light of the teaching of *eros* love at that time. That is, for Luther, God's love for human beings is certainly the foundation for human beings' love, but that love draws one not only to love one's neighbors but also to love God.

The principal difficulty in Lutheran theology in regard to the theme "love of God" lies in the fact that the Lutheran Reformation so strongly attacked the traditional medieval view that justifying faith was actually faith shaped by love (*fides caritate formata*). Problems with that lay in the misinterpretations that degraded the role of "faith alone" in justification and made love only a meritorious crown in the process.

In the following years, after his initial findings, Mannermaa conducted more research on Luther while serving as a professor at the theological faculty, and under his leadership and through his seminars, students studied Luther's writings and theology for their exams and thesis writing. Under his leadership, Finnish Luther research would begin its most intensive phase, during which more theologians would focus their work on Luther's theology.[6]

Mannermaa's pioneering work coincided with a fruitful collaboration between the Finnish Luther scholars and the Institut für Europäische Geschichte (Institute for European History) in Mainz and the Luther-Akademie (Luther Academy) in Ratzeburg. The increasing number of Finnish doctoral students involved in Luther research often worked as "Stipendiats" in Mainz and conducted research under the direction of both Professor Mannermaa and Professor Peter Manns (1924–1991), the director of the Abteilung Abendländische Religionsgeschichte des Mainzer Instituts (Department of the Western Religious History in Mainz), as well as Manns's colleague Dr. Rainer Vinke. Mannermaa and Manns had realized that they had both, in their own reading and lecturing of Luther's texts, come to parallel observations and criticism of the earlier interpretative traditions around Luther.

In the following, some of the independent monographs originating from this research network are introduced, in a chronological order. [For reasons of space limitations, only the first and foundational studies are characterized in more detail, whereas newer studies are simply introduced with a sentence or two.—Ed.]

Foundational Works

Juhani Forsberg (b. 1939), the author of this article, is Mannermaa's longtime assistant and colleague. He worked first as the first Finnish "Stipendiat" in Mainz and published a foundational study on Luther's interpretation of Abraham in 1984.[7] The idea to pursue this theme originated from Peter Manns, and the basic task was to answer the question of how Luther's theology was reflected in his exegesis on Abraham: how did Luther use the story of Abraham as a paradigm for his entire theology? As the central figure of the Old Testament, Abraham became for Luther most of all the paradigm for the gospel, and with that, for the doctrine of salvation, the concepts of faith, faith righteousness, hope and love, as well as for the church. Luther did not address all the aspects of Christian faith in his study of Abraham (for instance, he gave here only marginal attention to the concept of law), but themes such as the *absconditus* motif would prove to have a central place in Luther's Abraham exegesis, this so even if God spoke with Abraham from "mouth to mouth" ("von Mund zu Mund"; *de ore ad os*). To clarify, the concept of "*Deus absconditus*" here does not refer to "*deus nudus*" or "*deus in sua substantia*," which is beyond human comprehension. Rather, the *absconditus* motif in Luther's use is a positive and a revelatory-theological concept. The concept *absconditas Dei* is necessary precisely for revelatory purposes, because human beings could not bare an unveiled revelation of God. God reveals Godself to the human being, as in the case of Abraham, the most holy father of faith (*pater fidei sanctissimus*), only in the opposite (*sub contraria specie*). It is also worth noticing that Luther uses the concept "absence of God," "Verborgenheit" with two different meanings, which needs to be noted in any interpretation or use of the term.

Exegeting the biblical text, it is self-evident that the central issue Luther treats with the Abraham paradigm is the same as with the doctrine of justification. We could expect that the Abraham texts would lift up especially the imputative character of what happens in justification, but that is not exactly the case. Rather, in his Abraham exegesis, Luther talks about justification as the new creation, as the total change and righteousness-making, and gives only secondary attention to the forensic aspect of justification. The imputative aspect of justification, in light of these texts, means mainly that original sin is not taken into account. Even if the vocabulary in the Genesis lectures does not match word for word what is stated in

Luther's Galatians commentary, the actual doctrine of justification in both texts is identical. The analysis of Luther's Abraham exegesis thus supports Mannermaa's main interpretation.

The texts on Abraham allow Luther to conclude that the justification of the sinner brings about also a new reality of being, "*Seinswirklichkeit*," in the believer. This reality is not something we can understand with our reason or senses or mind—God's self-revelation is needed, and the believer can receive this only *sub contaria specie*. The motif of the theology of the cross thus runs through Luther's exegesis of Abraham. Furthermore, the *theologia crucis* holds a central place also in the theology of the mature Luther. Although when interpreted against the narrative exegesis on Abraham, something becomes manifest that was not that apparent or a concern at the time of writing the 1518 Heidelberg Disputation: the theology of the cross and the new "reality of being" are not opposite but rather belong together essentially.

Eero Huovinen (b. 1944), formerly professor of Dogmatics at the theological faculty at the University of Helsinki and, from 1991–2010, the bishop of Helsinki, has written two monographs on Luther's theology.[8] A colleague of Mannermaa, Huovinen wrote his thesis in the same scholarly network and climate at the same University of Helsinki. Also his interpretation reflects a certain "*Wirklichkeitsrealismus*," "actual realism," which is characteristic of Mannermaa and his school of thought.

Huovinen's study on the theology of death in Luther begins with addressing the traditionally established alternatives of "the immortality of the soul" or "the resurrection of the body." Outlining the different positions of Carl Stange, Anders Nygren, Karl Barth, and Leif Grane, Huovinen lifts up these writers' generally common approach to describe the relationship between human beings and God not ontologically but rather by using ethical and relational and personal concepts. This hermeneutical approach, however, does not do justice to Luther's theology of death, argues Huovinen. Moreover, "the immortality of the soul" and "the resurrection of the body" were actually not relevant alternatives for Luther, argues Huovinen.

Drawing on original sources from Luther, in particular his big Genesis commentary, Huovinen analyzed Luther's anthropology in light of the original state of humankind in creation and after the fall. He came to conclude that human beings, as images of God, were originally granted immortality as participation in the divine life. This participation did not belong in the realm of "possibility" (*potentia*) or qualities of human beings, something Luther himself criticized in scholastic anthropology, but instead he understood the participation as a "real-ontic" (that is, ontological and real) relationship between God and the human being. Even if the sin broke the original *imago Dei* in human beings, they could still through faith participate in immortality. Understanding death as "sleep," Luther did not consider it a total death for the justified human beings who, through and in Christ, whether in death or in the sleep of death, would continue to participate in godly life.

In his other Luther monograph, Huovinen examines Luther's teaching on the faith of a child or infant, *fides infantium*, and lifts up Luther's radical argument that newborn children receive their own faith. This theme has been studied before (for example, by the German Karl Brinkel in 1958), but Huovinen gives Luther's thinking here a new interpretation and both clarifies and corrects earlier findings. Huovinen cites many other scholars and their interpretations on Luther's idea of the faith of a child or infant. Huovinen takes a critical position with regard to those who consider the idea of an infant's faith as a more or less unfortunate postulate (for example, Paul Althaus, Helmut Thielicke, Erich Beyreuther, Otto Hermann Pesch, Peder Højen, Horst Kasten, Heino Falcke, and Hans Hubert), while finding complementary research elsewhere (by, for example, Ruben Josefson, Peter Brunner, Regin Prenter, and Lorenz Grönvik).

Huovinen would not accept the idea that the concept of an infant's faith was for Luther merely a helpful construction or a tool. Quite the contrary, Huovinen sees the idea of an infant's or child's faith as bound up with Luther's doctrine of *duplex iustitia*. Related to this argument, Huovinen posits that the "first kind of righteousness" in Luther's thinking has been actually grossly misinterpreted. According to Huovinen, in this particular context of explaining an infant's or child's faith, Luther actually gives a positive interpretation of *fides infusa*; the concept is necessary for understanding the possibility of an infant's faith, even if at the same time the reformer remains critical of the scholastics' teaching of *fides acquisita—fides infusa* in general. In Luther's understanding, posits Huovinen, the child's or infant's faith and the idea of *fides infusa* belong together. Furthermore, the child's or infant's faith effects a real participation in God and thus the beginning of the "second kind of righteousness" in the believer. Finally, in baptism, a child receives a *character indelebilis*, which means that baptism and its effects will last in eternity, "Ita eciam baptismus ineternum permanet."

[The work of Mannermaa, Forsberg, and Huovinen dates from the same period, each in its own right. Through their teaching, their publications, and their directing of dissertations, they have fostered an emerging school of Finnish Luther research that has a distinctive—even unique—voice.—Ed.]

The New Circle of Finnish Luther Research

Risto Saarinen (b. 1959), the successor of Mannermaa as Professor of Ecumenical Theology at the University of Helsinki, wrote his dissertation on the philosophical and hermeneutical issues in Luther research from the time of Neoprotestantism on.[9] He developed further Mannermaa's criticism of the problems in the interpretations (of, for example, Albrecht Ritschl, Adolf von Harnack, Wilhelm Hermann, and Karl Holl) that presume in Luther's thinking a division between "Being/Nature" (*Sein/Natur*) or "Religion/Ethics," which in neo-Kantian thinking (Hermann Lotze) depend on each other. These dynamics and lenses have lead to a misinterpretation of what Luther actually means by real-ontological. In these approaches, criticized by Saarinen, the relationship between human beings and God has become understood mainly as an ethical relation, in which the human will is to be oriented according to the divine will. Later Luther research of the early twentieth century (influenced by Karl Barth) came to appreciate Luther's theology as "actual" or "existential-theological" theology, and the word "ontological" (*ontologischen*) came to be understood in the framework of the ontology of "relations" or "persons." In his philosophical-hermeneutical analysis, Saarinen observes how "effect thinking" became fundamental in the ensuing Neoprotestant Luther scholarship. The dialectical theologians (Karl Barth and Ernst Wolf) who followed would end up distancing themselves not from this principle of "effect" necessarily but rather from Neoprotestantism's focus on Christ's work "for us" rather than Christ's presence "in us." Saarinen argues in favor of the value of "substance thinking" (*Substanzdenken*) and "effect thinking" (*Wirkungsdenken*) over Neoprotestant tendencies to reduce Luther's teaching of justification into some form of "ethicism" (*Ethicismus*). He also demonstrates that the assumptions about the basic differences between Protestant and Roman Catholic thinking have deep roots in this interpretative history and its problems. In light of his analysis, Saarinen concludes that the basic differences cannot really be assumed to exist in Luther's own theology.

Simo Peura (b. 1957), formerly from the University of Helsinki and a long-term collaborator with Mannermaa at the theology department there, and now the Bishop of Lapua in Finland, wrote his provocative dissertation on the concept of divinization (*Vergöttlichung, theosis, deificatio*). His thesis title is telling: *Mehr als ein Mensch?* (more than a human?).[10] Peura analyzes the use of the concept "divinization" in Luther's texts from 1513 to 1519 and tests Mannermaa's original argument in this light. His study is divided into three parts. Part 1 focuses on texts from 1513 to 1516 with the title "Vergöttlichung als geistliche Geburt in uns," divinization as a spiritual birth in us. The second part draws from Luther's commentary on Romans, with the title "Vergöttlichung im Kontext von Rechtfertigung und Gottesliebe," divinization in the context of justification and God's love. The third part addresses Luther's texts from 1517 to 1519, with the title "Vergöttlichung," divinization. More than examining Luther's use of the single term "divinization" in the approximately twenty instances we can find in all of his writings, the chapter actually pulls together several interrelated familiar topics that the concept of "divinization" draws organically together. In response to the critical question of how it was possible to take this rarely recognized term as the starting point to interpret Luther's entire theology—especially since the whole concept was alien to a majority of Luther scholars—Peura bases his argument on the *theologia crucis* and the central meaning of it for Luther himself.[11]

The concept "participation" (*Teilhabe, participatio*) includes essentially the very concept of divinization (*Vergottung*) as part of the explanation of the union (*unio*) between God and human beings in faith, hope, and love. Divinization is not at all an alien or a marginal concept in Luther's theology but rather serves the same cohesive purpose as it did already in patristic theology. Divinization does not mean any kind of apotheosis of human beings, as human beings remain as human beings and in themselves remain "nothing" (*Nichts*). With "more than a human" Peura means that human beings' participation in faith and love in Christ's self and in Christ's gift for us is possible and "effective" for us only under the sign of the cross. Peura concurs with the earlier studies that addressed Luther's ontology through the "real-ontic" thinking (Mannermaa 1989, 189–92) and as "ontology under the cross" (Forsberg 1984, 179). He proves that the concept of divinization and closely related issues are not limited only to the pre-reformation thinking of the "young" Luther.

[After the studies of Saarinen and Peura, several new works were and are being published. In the following, only three of these are characterized briefly, with the others simply mentioned, even if each of them merits more space, as in the original article.—Ed.]

Antti Raunio (b. 1958), of the department of Theology at the University of Helsinki, wrote his dissertation on the golden rule in Luther's theology.[12] The first part of the study, titled "Das Verhältnis zwischen natürlichem Gesetz und göttlicher Liebe" (The Relationship between Natural Law and Divine Love), surveys Luther's interpretation of the golden rule in his earliest works. Then follows an analysis of the young Luther and his lectures on Romans, before the work concludes with the study of Luther's texts from 1517 to 1527. Adding to the earlier Finnish study by Jorma Laulaja on the golden rule as Luther's social-ethical maxim,[13] Raunio argues for a much larger role of the golden rule in Luther's theology. More than an ethical or social-ethical maxim, it is an essential part of understanding God-human relationship; that is, it has a place in understanding the justification of human beings in relation to God as well as in relation to human beings' love for God. Faith is the fulfillment of the golden rule, and life under that rule is to be understood in light of theology of the cross. The golden rule is part of Luther's thinking about how God in God's *agape* love deals with human beings: the sanctifying and saving work of Christ, Christ's becoming human and his redeeming work, can be understood as the fulfillment of the golden rule.

Mannermaa's study of the Heidelberg Disputation had addressed the difference between human and divine love as a central structure of Luther's theology. He had lifted up the notion that the characteristic of divine love was that it created "what is" from "what is not." This would be pursued further in other works under Mannermaa's guidance.

Sammeli Juntunen (b. 1964), of the department of Theology at the University of Helsinki and currently a senior pastor in Savonlinna, wrote his dissertation on the concept of "nothingness" and "annihilation" (*Nichts* and *annihilatio*) in Luther's theology.[14] The first part of his voluminous study gives an overview of the use of the term *nihil* in the philosophical tradition before Luther, from antiquity and early Christian theology to scholastic theology and medieval mysticism, leading up to Luther's most important teachers at Erfurt University. The main part of the study is arranged chronologically: the study surveys the earliest writings of Luther from 1515 to 1518 and 1519 to 1523. The lectures on the Psalms are at the center stage during the first period, whereas lectures on Romans, together with the Heidelberg Disputation, are at the focus of the second part. The third part focuses on the second Psalms lectures, *The Magnificat*, and selected sermons.

Already in the first period, we can see the most important terms being in use with Luther: "nothingness" (*Nichts*) in the formulations of "*nihil ex se*" and "*annihilatio*" or annihilation of the human being. In the second period, the term *annihilatio* is used in relation to the human being's form (*forma*) as a sinner. The third period brings to use the expression "*redigere ad nihilum*." The chronological survey shows no fundamental development in Luther's use of the term "nothingness" between 1510 and 1523.

To summarize Juntunen's findings: When Luther states that human beings are *nihil*, he means that human beings are dependent on God both naturally and existentially in the ontological sense. This "nothingness," however, does not make the real presence of Christ in faith impossible. Just as Christ has become "nothing," human beings receive a new being in the participation in Christ and in all Christ's goods (*bona*). In this participation the human being stands opposite to God's love that is oriented toward that "which is not" in order to create good out of nothingness. To be made Christ means to be the object of God's creating and justifying love. Christ is a human who is *nihil ex se* and through the alien work of God (*opus alienum dei*) is being constantly made into nothing (*annihilatio, redactio ad nihilum*). The sin and sins are nothing in front of God (*nihil coram deo*), as they have no being in Christ. The *forma* of the natural human being, that is, concupiscence, becomes destroyed in justification and established with a new form, *forma*, that is, Christ. This ontologically radical change in human being is called *annihilatio*. The natural human being who in his or her love only seeks what he or she considers good, must not only consider the neighbor's sins as nothing but also appreciate God in God's negative being (*negativa essentia*), because God appears to them in the opposite of what the natural human beings would consider as "good" or as that "which is."

Referring to earlier works dealing with Luther's understanding of the "relational-personal" and "nothingness," "*nihil*," and "annihilation" (Gerhard Ebeling and Wilfried Joest), Juntunen moves on to examine what kind of an inner reality follows from the annihilating work of Christ and how the reality of grace is manifested in external relations. Juntunen concludes from Luther that when human beings are made into nothing in front of God, they at the same time become participants of Christ and through that are made into *nova creatura*. This means that as new creatures, human beings receive from God's *agape* love not only their natural *esse* but also their new spiritual *esse,* and this through the union of faith with Christ. Luther binds together the two meanings of *substantia* in the tradition of the patristic theologians: For Luther, human being becomes "Christ" in faith, the spiritual *substantia extrinseca*, and this Christ then becomes human beings' spiritual *subsistentia seu essentia intrinseca*.

Kari Kopperi (b. 1960), in his dissertation, offered a thorough analysis of Luther's theological and philosophical theses in the

Heidelberg Disputation.[15] Kopperi criticizes earlier interpretations of the Heidelberg Disputation and its theology of the cross, and he points out the connection between Luther's theology of the cross and Luther's theology of love. Namely, in Luther's late medieval theological context, the question of "pure" love for God was the central issue, and it was Luther's realization of the impossibility for human beings' to offer "pure" love for God that led him into distinguishing between God's love and human love. This distinction is at the heart of his theology of the cross. Thesis 28 holds the key in both regards.

In his conclusion, Kopperi points out that the intention of the philosophical theses in the disputation can only be understood correct if interpreted theologically. That is, Luther's intention was to point out how Aristotle's philosophy cannot assist Christian theology, not to dismiss the importance of philosophy per se. With his paradoxical thesis, Luther moved away from the *facere quod in se est* and "merit" thinking, away from the belief in free will and Pelagianism, and away from the theology of glory. Right theology, for Luther, is based on God's love, which is manifested to human beings in the cross of Christ and is beyond human understanding until the coming revelation of the cross.

Other Noteworthy Studies: Dissertations and Beyond

Among other noteworthy recent studies, the following works can be lifted up as charting new waters: Pekka Kärkkäinen (b. 1967), in his dissertation, explored Luther's theology of the Holy Spirit in light of trinitarian doctrine and as related to Luther's understanding of the sacraments, ecclesiology, and the Bible, and central christological concepts (such as *communicatio idiomatum*).[16] Olli-Pekka Vainio's (b. 1976) dissertation surveyed both Luther's theology and the development of the doctrine of justification from Luther to the writers of the Formula of Concord. He demonstrated that, amid the varied emphasis among the reformers in their explanations of justification (and regarding its two poles, forensic versus effective, in particular), there is an evident agreement on the effectiveness of faith in justification, "Wirklichkeit des Glaubens" (*forma fidei*), which results in a distinctive Lutheran teaching of justification.[17] Jari Jolkkonen's (b. 1970) doctoral work examined Luther's teaching of the Lord's Supper and its practice in his time, and the interrelatedness of the doctrine and practice in that regard.[18]

In addition to explicitly Luther-centered dissertations, other types of works have been published as well, dissertations and beyond. For instance, Miikka Ruokanen (b. 1953), professor of Dogmatic Theology at the University of Helsinki, has written on Luther's understanding of Holy Scripture, among other studies.[19] Kalevi Tanskanen (b. 1936) wrote his dissertation on the ethics of economy in Luther and in the Middle Ages.[20] Eeva Martikainen (b. 1949 d. 2010), professor of Systematic Theology at the University of Joensuu, has published a small monograph on Luther's understanding of doctrine.[21] In Swedish-speaking scholarly circles in Finland, at the University of Turku (Åbo Akademi), a long tradition of Luther research has been maintained by, for instance, Fredric Cleve (b. 1930) and Lorenz Grönvik (b. 1930). Hans-Olof Kvist (b. 1941), professor of Systematic Theology in Turku, has written several articles on Reformation theology, and, more recently, Bernice Sundkvist (b. 1956) has written a dissertation on the sacramental character of Luther's proclamation.[22] Kaarlo Arffman (b. 1950), a church historian with a different specialty from that of the systematicians in Finland, and a prolific writer, has published several works touching upon Luther and the Reformation. His dissertation on the universities and magistrates at the beginning of the Reformation[23] has led to a variety of writings on Luther and Lutheran themes.[24] Several other Luther-related studies have been published or are in the process of being published, too many to list here.

In sum, Finnish Luther research since 1979 has produced thousands of pages of scholarly publications, mostly in the form of dissertations. What the long-term impact of these works in the international community of Luther scholars might be remains to be seen; time will tell. Already having elicited both excitement and criticism, the findings from Finland have stirred considerable interest around the world. Debate and discussion are a crucial part of all scholarship, and the future will show how successful and long-lasting Finnish Luther research turns out to be, and in what directions it leads.

Luther's Works Cited

Collected Works

D. Martin Luther's Werke. Kritische Gesamtausgabe. Weimar: Böhlaus, 1906–1961. (Weimar Ausgabe, Weimar Edition. Abbreviated WA.)

Luther's Works, American Edition. Edited by Jaroslav Pelikan and Helmut T. Lehmann. 55 vols. St. Louis: Concordia; Philadelphia: Fortress Press, 1955–1986. (Abbreviated LW).

Individual Texts in Luther's Works and the Weimar Edition

Heidelberg Disputation, 1518. In *Career of the Reformer* 1. Edited by Harold J. Grimm. LW 31:35–70. Philadelphia: Fortress Press, 1957. WA 1.

The Freedom of a Christian, 1520. In *Career of the Reformer* 1. Edited by Harold J. Grimm. LW 31:327–77. Philadelphia: Fortress Press, 1957. WA 7.

Lectures on Romans. Edited by Hilton C. Oswald. LW 25. St. Louis: Concordia, 1972. WA 56:4–31.

The Magnificat, 1521. In *The Sermon on the Mount and The Magnificat.* Edited by Jaroslav Pelikan. LW 21:295–358. St. Louis: Concordia, 1956. WA 7.

Lectures on Galatians: Chapters 1–4, 1535. Edited by Jaroslav Pelikan and Walter A. Hansen. LW 26. St. Louis: Concordia, 1963. WA 40/1.

Lectures on Galatians: Chapters 5–6, 1535, and Lectures on Galatians, Chapters 1–6, 1519. Edited by Jaroslav Pelikan and Daniel E. Poellot. LW 27:3–149. St. Louis: Concordia, 1964. WA 40/2.

"Psalm 117." In *Selected Psalms* 3. Edited by Jaroslav Pelikan and Walter A. Hansen. LW 14:1–39. St. Louis: Concordia, 1958. WA 31/1.

Against Latomus, 1521. In *Career of the Reformer* 2. Edited by George W. Forell. LW 32:133–260. Philadelphia: Fortress Press, 1958. WA 9.

Lectures on Genesis: Chapters 21–25. Edited by Jaroslav Pelikan and Walter A. Hansen. LW 4. St. Louis: Concordia, 1964. WA 43.

Treatise on Good Works, 1520. In *The Christian in Society* 1. Edited by James Atkinson. LW 44:15–114. Philadelphia: Fortress Press, 1966. WA 6.

First Lectures on the Psalms 2. Edited by Hilton C. Oswald. LW 11. St. Louis: Concordia, 1976. WA 4.

Individual Texts in the Weimar Edition

"In Natali Christi." Christmas Sermon, 1515. WA 1.

Vorlesung über Jesaias (Lectures on Isaiah), 1527–1530. WA 31/2.

Crucigers Sommerpostille (Cruciger's Summer Postil), 1544. WA 21.

Kirchenpostille (Church Postil), 1522. WA 10/1.

Operationes in psalmos, 1518–1521. WA 5.

Erste Antinomer Disputation (First Disputation against the Antinomians), 1537. WA 39.

Adventspostille (Advent Postil) 1522. WA 10.

Fastenpostille (Lenten Postil), 1525. WA 17/2.

Resolutiones disputationum de indulgentiarum virtute (Disputation on the Value of Indulgences), 1518. WA 1.

Christliche Schrift, sich in den ehelichen Stand zu begeben (Christian Scripture regarding the State of Marriage), 1525. WA 18.

Wider den falsch genannten geistlichen Stand des Papstes und der Bischöfe (Against the Falsely Called Spiritual Estate of the Papacy and the Bishops). WA 10/2.

"Predigt" (Sermon), 1522. WA 10/3.

Notes

Chapter 1: Love for "What Is" and Love for "What Is Not"

1. The best available edition of the Heidelberg Disputation (1518) is found in *Studienausgabe* 1, trans. H.-U. Delius (Berlin, 1979) (abbreviated *Sta* 1). See *Sta* 1:213, 27–28. For the English translation in Luther's Works, American Edition (LW), based on the Latin text in the Weimar edition (WA) 1:353–74, see Heidelberg Disputation, LW 31:39–58.

2. [For clarity's sake, when the word "love" is used to describe the difference between "human love" and "love of God" or "God's love," the terms are capitalized, as in "Human Love" and "God's Love." This is an editorial addition to better highlight the central emphasis and argument.—Ed.]

3. Heidelberg Disputation (1518), LW 31:57. "Amor Dei non inuenit, sed creat suum diligibile, Amor hominis fit a suo diligibili." *Sta* 1:212, 1–3; WA 1:365, 2ff. [Translated by the author and the translator.—Ed.]

4. *Sta* 1:212, 15–16; WA 1:365, 16–17. "Beatus qui intelligit super egemum (et) pauperem." Heidelberg Disputation, LW 31:57. The quotation from Psalm 41 is based on the Vulgate. [Translated by the author and the translator.—Ed.]

5. [When talking about God, whose way of "being," "essence," "nature," and "substance" remain veiled to human mind and language, extra care is needed in word choices. For the Finnish original "olemus," which could be translated "form of being," the words "being" and "essence" convey the meaning best.—Ed.]

6. Heidelberg Disputation, LW 31:57. "Ideo enim peccatores sunt pulchri, quia diliguntur, non ideo diliguntur, quia sunt pulchri." *Sta* 1:212, 10–11; WA 1:365, 11f. [Translated by the author and the translator.—Ed.]

7. Heidelberg Disputation, LW 31:57. "Et iste est amor crucis ex cruce natus, qui illuc sese transfert, non ubi inuenit bonum quo fruatur, sed ubi bonum conferat malo (et) egeno." *Sta* 1:212, 10–11; WA 1:365, 13–15.

8. *The Magnificat* (1521), LW 21:299; WA 7:547, 1–10. [LW here unnecessarily uses masculine pronouns for God; the Finnish language uses a neutral pronoun for God and human beings, "hän." In this work, some LW translations are revised in this regard. —Ed.]

9. *The Magnificat*, LW 21:300, WA 7:547, 17–32.

10. E.g., *Rationis Latomianae confutatio* (1521), *Studienausgabe* 2:441, 4–7; WA 8:65, 8–10; *Against Latomus* (1521), LW 32:169–70.

11. See Heiko O. Oberman, *Luther: Mensch zwischen Gott und Teufel* (Berlin, 1981), 286–90; *Luther: Man between God and the Devil*, trans. Eileen Walliser-Schwarzbart (New Haven & London: Yale University Press, 1989).

12. *Lectures on Galatians* (1535), LW 27:58; WA 40/2:72, 5–6 (cf. 31–36).

Chapter 2: Two Kinds of Love and Love as a Unifying Power

1. [The term "unify" may better convey the actual meaning here, even if in English the words "unite" and "uniting" might at times sound better. In the following, both words are used to describe the idea of "being united" and "becoming one" and "unified" when translating the Finnish word "*yhdistää*" and its equivalents.—Ed.]

2. The words "appetitive" (cf. Latin *appetitus*, "desire toward") and the noun "appetite" are used in this work as neutral terms for "desiring" and "desire" and "desiring love," without the connotations of *amor concupiscentiae*, concupiscent love.

3. A reader familiar with our topic will be aware of both the extent to which Anders Nygren's interpretation of the relationship between *eros* and *agape* is accepted in this study and also of the extent to which this interpretation is rejected here. See Anders Nygren, *Agape and Eros*; trans. Philip S. Watson (London: SPCK, 1953). Nygren does not recognize *unio* in the context of the *agape* motif. Another significant history of the concept of love is that of Helmut Kuhn, *Liebe: Geschichte eines Begriffes* (Munich, 1975). Luther, however, is barely mentioned in this work.

4. *Lectures on Romans* (1515–1516), LW 25:513–14; WA 56:518, 4–31.

5. E.g., Thomas Aquinas, *Summa theologiae* (*Sth*) 2-2.q.25.a.4.c., in R. J. Batten O.P., the "Blackfriars English edition" of *Summa theologiae*; trans. Thomas Gilby et al.; 60 vols. (London: Eyre and Spottiswoode, and New York: McGraw-Hill, 1964–1973). [The following references to *Sth* 2-2 refer to this Blackfriars English edition.—Ed.]

6. [The Finnish expression "*uskon maailma*," difficult to translate precisely, is a broad term entailing dimensions from theology, spirituality, piety, religious beliefs, and other aspects pertaining to persons' religious views and faith life.—Ed.]

7. "Propter amorem boni omnia agunt quaecumque agunt." *Sth*. 1-2.q.28.a.6. in Eric D'Arcy, the "Blackfriars English edition" of *Summa theologiae*.

8. See, e.g., *Sth*. 1-2.q.26.a.1 (D'Arcy).

9. See *Sth*. 1-2.q.27.a.3 (D'Arcy).

10. *Sth*. 1-2.q.26.a.1 (D'Arcy).

11. E.g., *Sth*. 1.q.81 (Batten).

12. *Sth*. 1-2.q.26.a.2 (Batten).

13. *Sth*. 1-2.q.26.a.2.c (D'Arcy).

14. *Sth*. 1-2.q.27.a.3 (D'Arcy); *CG* 4:19.

15. Bernhardt Ziermann, *Kommentar: Die deutsche Thomas-Ausgabe* (Graz, 1955), 10:533.

16. *Sth*. 1-2.q.26.a.4; *Sth*. 1-2.q.27.a.3 (D'Arcy).

17. *Sth*. 1-2.q.26.a.4 (D'Arcy).

18. *Sth*. 2-2.q.23.a.1 (Batten).

19. *Sth*. 2-2.q.23.a.1 (Batten).

20. *Sth*. 1-2.q.26.a.4.c (D'Arcy).

21. *Sth*. 22.q.23.a.4.c (Batten).

22. *Sth*. 2-2.q.25.a.4.c (Batten).

23. Ziermann, *Kommentar*, 539.

24. E.g., *Sth*. 1.q.20.a.1 (D'Arcy). See also Kuhn, *Liebe*, 134.

25. *Sth*. 1.q.20.a.4 (D'Arcy).

26. *CG* 3.q.17; *Sth*. 1.q.60.a.5; 3. *Sent*. 29.1.

27. *Sth*. 2-2.q.24.a.9.c (Batten).

28. *Entelekeia*, the state where the end has already been reached, that is, full or complete reality.

29. Karl-Heinz zur Mühlen, *Reformatorische Vernunftkritik und neuzeitliches Denken* (Tübingen, 1980), 14.

30. "Sicut etiam videmus in motu corporali quod primum est recessus a termino; secundum autem est appropinquatio ad alium terminum; tertium autem quies in termino." *Sth.* 2-2.q.24.a.9.c (English translation: R. J. Batten O.P., the Blackfriars edition of *Summa theologiae*).

31. "Et hoc pertinet ad perfectos, qui 'cupiunt dissolvi et esse cum Christo.'" Ibid.; the English translation of Phil. 1:23 is from the Blackfriars edition of *Summa theologiae*.

32. *Lectures on Galatians* (1535), LW 26:129. "Nos autem loco charitatis istius ponimus fidem." WA 40/1:228, 27.

33. Heidelberg Disputation, LW 31:57. ". . . illuc sese transfert, non ubi inuenit bonum quo fruatur, sed ubi bonum conferat malo (et) egeno." *Sta* 1:212, 13–14; WA 1:365, 14–15.

34. *First Lectures on the Psalms* 2, LW 11:403. "Hoc est esse deum: non accipere bona, sed dare." *Dictata super Psalterium* (1513–1516), WA 4:269, 25–26. [Translated by the author and the translator.—Ed.]

35. This is the main content in the summary of Luther's theology as presented in *The Freedom of a Christian*, LW 31:333–77; WA 7:12–73.

36. *Lectures on Romans* (1515–1516), LW 25:513–14; WA 56:518, 4–31.

37. "Nu gibt dis gepott eyn recht lebendig exempel, nemlich dich selbs, das exempel ist ia edler denn aller heyligen exempel. Denn die selben sind vergangen und nu todt. Dis exempel aber lebet on unterlas. Denn es wird yhe yderman muessen bekennen, das er fule, wie er sich liebet. Er fulet ia, wie hefftig er fur seyn leben sorget, wie vleyssig er seynes leybs wartet mit speys, kleyder und allem guet, wie er den tod fleucht und alles ungluck meydet. Nu das ist liebe deyns selbs, die sihestu und fulestu. Was leret dich nu dis gebott? eben dasselb gleich zuthuen, das du dir thuest, das du seyn leyb und leben sollt dyr gleich so viel lassen gelten als deyn leyb und leben. Sihe, wie hette er dyr kund eyn neher, lebendiger und krefftiger exempel geben, das ynn dyr selb so tieff stickt, ia du selber bist." *Fastenpostille* (Lenten Postil) (1525), WA 17/2:102, 27–39. [Words such as "*muessen*," "*zuthuen*," and "*thuest*" are rendered here with letters available in English. The same practice is followed in the ensuing notes as needed.—Ed.]

38. See, e.g., *Erste Antinomer Disputation* (1537), WA 39 1:361, 19–20. For a fundamental work on Luther's theology of the law, see Lauri Haikola, *Usus legis* (Helsinki, 1981).

39. See Jorma Laulaja, "Kultaisen säännön etiikka: Lutherin sosiaalietiikan luonnonoikeudellinen perusstruktuuri" [The Ethics of the golden rule. The Basic Structure of Luther's Social Ethics in the Light of Natural Law] (diss., Helsinki, 1981), with a German abstract.

40. *Adventspostille* (Advent Postil) (1522), WA 10/1/2:42, 21—43, 4.

Chapter 3: The Theology of Glory versus the Theology of the Cross

1. Heidelberg Disputation, LW 31:52–53. "XIX. Non ille digne Theologus dicitur, qui invisibilia Dei, per ea, quae facta sunt, intellecta conspicit.

"Patet per eos, qui tales fuerunt Et tamen ab Apostolo Roma. I. stulti vocantur. Porro invisibilia Dei sunt, virtus, divinitas sapientia, iusticia, bonitas et cetera. haec omnia cognita non faciunt dignum, nec sapientem.

"XX. Sed qui visibilia et posteriora Dei, per passiones et crucem conspecta intelligit.

"Posteriora et visibilia Dei sunt opposita invisibilium, id est, humanitas, infirmitas, stulticia, Sicut I. Corinth. I. vocat infirmum et stultum Dei, Quia enim homines cognitione Dei ex operibus abusi sunt, voluit rursus Deus ex passionibus cognosci et reprobare illam sapientiam invisibilium, per sapientiam visibilium, ut sic, qui Deum non coluerunt manifestum ex operibus, colerent absconditum in passionibus, Sicut ait I. Corinth. I. Quia in Dei sapientia non cognovit mundus Deum per sapientiam, placuit

Deo per stulticiam praedicationis salvos facere credentes, Ita, ut nulli iam satis sit ac prosit, qui cognoscit Deum in gloria et maiestate, nisi cognoscat eundem in humilitate et ignominia crucis. Sic perdit sapientiam sapientum et cetera. sicut Isaias dicit: Vere absconditus tu es Deus.

"Sic Iohan. 14. Cum Philippus iuxta Theologiam gloriae diceret: Ostende nobis Patrem, mox Christus retraxit et in seipsum reduxit eius volatilem cogitatum querendi Deum alibi, dicens: Philippe, qui videt me, videt et patrem meum. Ergo in Christo crucifixo est vera Theologia et cognitio Dei. . . .

"XXI. Theologus gloriae dicit, Malum bonum, et bonum malum, Theologus crucis dicit, id quod res est.

"Patet, quia dum ignorat Christum, igorat Deum absconditum in passionibus. Ideo praefert opera passionibus, et gloriam cruci, potentiam infirmitati, sapientiam stulticiae, et universaliter bonum malo." *Sta* 1:207, 25—208, 24; WA 1:361, 31—362, 25. [The translation is by the author and the translator and differs in nuance from that in LW. These changes are significant, considering the importance of this text for Mannermaa's full argumentation.—Ed.]

2. "Theologus vero gloriae . . . discit ex Aristotele, quod obiectum voluntatis sit bonum et bonum amabile, malum vero odibile, ideo deum esse summum bonum et summe amabile." *Resolutiones disputationum de indulgentiarum virtute* (1518); WA 1:614, 17–22.

3. Heidelberg Disputation, LW 31:52. "XIX. Non ille digne Theologus dicitur, qui invisibilia Dei, per ea, quae facta sunt, intellecta conspicit." *Sta* 1:207, 26–27; WA 1:361, 32–33. [Translated by the author and the translator.—Ed.]

4. See, e.g., Walter Brugger S.J., *Theologia naturalis* (Institutiones philosophiae scholasticiae 6) (Barcelona, 1964), 254f.

5. *Lectures on Genesis* (1535), LW 4:145. "Non enim aliam notitiam de Deo habent, quam Philosophicam aut metaphysicam. Quod Deus est ens separatum a creaturis, ut ait Aristoteles, verax, intra se contemplans creaturas. Sed quid haec ad nos? Diabolus etiam sic Deum cognoscit, et scit esse veracem, sed in Theologia quando de agnitione Dei docetur, agnoscendus et appraehendus est Deus, non intra se manens, sed ab extra veniens ad nos, ut videlicet statuamus eum nobis esse Deum. // Ille prior Aristotelicus vel Philosophicus Deus Iudaeorum, Turcarum, Papistarum Deus est, nihil vero is ad nos." WA 43:240, 22–30. [The translation is revised with respect to unnecessary masculine pronouns. —Ed.]

6. Exod. 33:23.

7. On fuller development of Luther's concept of Christ as the "greatest sinner" and the doctrine of justification, see Tuomo Mannermaa, *Christ Present in Faith: Luther's View of Justification* (Minneapolis: Fortress Press, 2005).

8. See Heidelberg Disputation, *Sta* 1, 201, 27–28; WA 1:357, 6–8; LW 31:44. On Luther's view of God's wrath, see Lennart Pinomaa, *Der Zorn Gottes in der Theologie Luthers* (Helsinki, 1938).

9. *Lectures on Romans* (1515–1516), LW 25:418–19. "Deus Non saluat nisi peccatores, Non erudit nisi stultos et insipientes, Non ditat nisi pauperes, Non Uiuificat nisi mortuos; Non eos quidem, qui se tales fingunt aut reputant solum, Sed qui vere tales sunt et hoc agnoscunt." WA 56:427, 1–6. [The translation is revised with respect to unnecessary masculine pronouns.—Ed.]

10. Heidelberg Disputation, LW 31:44. "Opera Dei esse deformia, patet per illud Esa. 53. Non est ei species neq(ue) decor, Et I. Reg. 2. Dominus mortificat (et) vivificat, deducit ad inferos et reducit. Hoc sic intelligitur, quod Dominus humiliat et perterrefacit nos Lege et conspectu peccatorum nostrorum, ut tam coram hominibus, quam coram nobis videamur esse nihil, stulti, mali, imo vere tales sumus. Quod cum agnoscimus

atque confitemur, nulla in nobis est species neque decor, sed vivimus in abscondito Dei (id est, in nuda fiducia misericordiae eius) in nobis habentes responsum peccati, stulticiae, mortis et inferni, Iuxta illud Apostoli, 2. Corinth. 6. Quasi tristes, semper autem gaudentes, quasi mortui, et ecce vivimus. Et hoc est, quod Esaias cap. 28. vocat, opus alienum Dei, ut operetur opus suum (id est, nos humiliat in nobis, desperantes faciens, ut exaltet in sua misericordia, sperantes faciens), Sicut Hab. 3. Cum iratus fueris, misericordiae recordaberis. Talis ergo homo sibi displicet in omnibus operibus suis, nullum decorem, sed solam suam deformitatem videt. Imo etiam foris facit, quae aliis stulta et deformia videntur." *Sta* 1:201, 19—202, 4; WA 1:356, 35—357, 4. [The translation here is slightly revised to reflect the rendering in the original Finnish and in the WA.—Ed.]

11. *Lectures on Romans*, LW 25:204. "Vbi 'non est opus medico nisi male habentibus', Non queritur ouis nisi quae periit, Non liberatur nisi captiuus, Non locupletatur nisi pauper, non Roboratur nisi infirmus, non exaltatur nisi humiliatus, Non impletur nisi quod vacuum est, Non construitur nisi quod inconstructum est. Et Vt philosophi dicunt: Non inducitur forma, nisi vbi est priuatio forme precedentisque expulsio, Et: intellectus possibilis non recipit formam, nisi in principio sui esse sit nudatus ab omni forma et sicut tabula rasa." WA 56:218, 17—219, 2. [The translation is slightly revised so as to reflect the original.—Ed.]

12. *Lectures on Romans*, LW 25:367. "Ière. 23.: 'In Nouissimis intelligetis consilium eius,' q.d. In principio seu primo nostrum intelligimus, Sed in vltimo Dei consilium intelligimus. / Iohann. 14.: 'Cum factum fuerit, credatis.' / Quia, Vt dixi, Sicut artifex fertur super materiam abilem et aptam ad opus artis suae formandum, Que aptitudo materiae Est quedam insensata oratio pro forma, quam artifex intelligit et exaudit, dum facere disponit, quod illa aptitudine sua querit, Ita Deus fertur super nostrum affectum et cogitatum Videns, quid petat, ad quid sese aptet et quid desyderet; tunc exaudiens incipit artis et consilii sui formam imprimere. Vbi necessario perit forma et Idea cogitationis nostrae. Sic Genes. 1.: 'Spiritus Domini ferebatur super aquas Et tenebrae erant super faciem abyssi.' Nota: 'super faciem abyssi' dicit, non 'super abyssum', quia secundum speciem apparet nobis aduersum, quando spiritus super nos fertur facturus, quod petimus." WA 56:377, 24—378, 12. [The translation is revised with respect to unnecessary masculine pronouns. —Ed.]

13. "Ita semper perit semperque servatur pius." *Operationes in psalmos* (1518–1521), WA 5:444, 25. [The translation here is by the author and the translator. —Ed.]

14. *Lectures on Romans*, LW 25:382–83. "Bonum enim nostrum absconditum est et ita profunde, Vt sub contrario absconditum sit. Sic Vita nostra sub morte, dilectio nostri sub odio nostri, gloria sub ignominia, salus sub perditione, regnum sub exilio, celum sub inferno, sapientia sub stultia, Iustitia sub peccato, virtus sub infirmitate. Et vniversaliter omnis nostra affirmatio boni cuiuscunque sub negatione eiusdem, Vt fides locum habeat in Deo, Qui Est Negativa Essentia et bonitas et Sapientia et Iustitia Nec potest possideri aut attingi nisi negatis omnibus affirmatiuis nostris." WA 56:392, 28—393, 3.

15. *Selected Psalms* 3 (Ps. 117; 1530), LW 14:31. "Die gnade scheinet eusserlich, als sey es eitel zorn, so tieff ligt sie verborgen mit den zweyen dicken fellen odder heuten zugedeckt, Nemlich das sie unser widder teil und die welt verdamnen und meiden als eine plage und zorn Gottes, Und wir selbs auch nicht anders fulen ynn uns, das wol Petrus sagt, Allein das wort leuchte uns wie ynn einem finstern ort. Ja freylich ein finster ort. Also mus Gottes trew und warheit auch ymer dar zuvor eine grosse lugen werden, ehe sie zur warheit wird. Denn fur der wellt heist sie eine Ketzerey. So dunckt uns auch delbs ymer dar, Got wolle uns lassen und sein wort nicht halten und sehet an ynn unserm hertzen ein lugener zu werden. Und Summa, Got kan nicht Got sein, Er mus zuvor ein Teufel werden, und wir konnen nicht gen himel komen, wir mussen vorhin ynn die helle faren, konnen nicht Gottes kinder werden, wir werden denn zuvor des

Teufels kinder. Denn alles was Got redet und thut, das mus der Teufel geredt und gethan haben. Und unser fleisch hellts selbs auch dafur, das uns genaw und nehrlich der geist ym wort erhellt und anders gleuben leret. Widderumb aber der welt lugen kan nicht zur lugen werden, sie mus zuvor die warheit werden, Und die Gottlosen faren nicht ynn die helle, sie seyen denn zuvor ynn den himel gefaren und werden nicht des Teufels kinder, sie mussen zuvor Gottes kinder sein." WA 31/1:249, 16—250, 2. [The translation is revised with respect to unnecessary masculine pronouns. —Ed.]

16. *Selected Psalms* 3 (Ps. 117), LW 14:32. "Und Summa, der Teuffel wird und ist kein Teuffel, er sey denn zuvor Gott gewest. Er wird kein Engel der finsternis, Er sey denn zuvor ein Engel des liechts worden. Denn was der Teuffel redet und thut, das mus Gott gered und gethan haben, das gleubt die welt und bewegt uns wol selber. Daruemb ists hoch gered und mus hoher verstand hie sein, das Gottes gnade und wahrheit odder seine guete und trew walte uber uns und oblige. Aber troestlich ists, wers fassen kan, wenn er gewis ist, das es Gottes gnade und trew ist, und doch sich anders ansehen lesst und mit geistlichem trotz sagen koenne: Wolan, ich weis vorhin wol, das Gottes wort eine grosse luegen werden mus auch jnn mir selbs, ehe es die wahrheit wird. Widderuemb weis ich, das des Teuffels wort mus zuvor die zarte Goettliche warheit werden ehe sie zur luegen wird. Ich mus dem Teuffel ein stuendlein die Gottheit goennen, und unsern Gott die Teuffelheit zuschreiben lassen. Es ist aber damit noch nicht alle tage abent. Es heisst doch zuletzt: seine guete und trew waltet uber uns." WA 31/1:250, 24–37. [Here several words, such as "*guete*," "*luegen*," and "*troestlich*" are rendered with English letters. The translation is revised with respect to unnecessary masculine pronouns. —Ed.]

17. *Lectures on Romans*, LW 25:365. "Inde enim fit, Quod cum petimus Deum, quaecunque illa tandem sint, Et ipse exaudiens incipit ea velle donare, Sic donat, ut contraveniat omnibus nostris conceptibus i.e. cogitationibus, ita vt appareat nobis post petitiones magis offensum esse et minus fieri ea, que petimus, quam ante. Quod totum ideo facit, Quia Natura Dei est, prius destruere et annihilare, quicquid in nobis est, antequam sua donet; sicut Scriptum est: 'Dominus pauperem facit et ditat, deducit ad inferos et reducit.'" WA 56:375, 14–20. [The translation is revised with respect to unnecessary masculine pronouns. —Ed.]

18. *Lectures on Romans*, LW 25:370. "Sed nonne et passim predicamus Magnam et miram esse Dei potentiam, Sapientiam, bonitatem, Iustitiam, misericordiam, et non intelligimus? Quia metaphysice intelligimus, i.e. secundum quod nos eas comprehendimus scil. apparentes et non absconditas, Cum suam potentiam non nisi sub infirmitate, Sapientiam sub stultitia, Bonitatem sub austeritate, Iustitiam sub peccatis, misericordiam sub ira absconderit. Inde non intelligunt Dei potentiam, quando vident infirmitatem etc. Sic psalmo 80.: 'Exaudivi te in abscondito tempestatis.' Ecce 'in abscondito', quod est: quando tempestas irae abscondit dulcedinem misericordie, i.e. quando nos exaudit in contraria operatione nostris cogitationibus. Nos petimus salutem, et ipse, ut saluet, amplius infert damnationem, et sub tali tempestate abscondit suam exauditionem. Vt figuratum est Exo. 3., Quando incepit populum velle liberare, fortius suscitauit Pharaonem contra illum, ut minus liberare velle videretur." WA 56:380, 31—381, 8.

19. *Against Latomus* (1521), LW 32:169–70. "Est quide(m) synecdoche dulcissima (et) necessaria figura (et) charitatis misericordiaeq(ue) dei symbolu(m), vt dum percutere aliquando dicitur aut vastare, no(n) penitus delere aut omnes percutere intelligat(ur), totum enim tangit, quando parte(m) eius tangit." *Sta* 2:441, 4–7; WA 8:65, 8–10.

20. *Lectures on Galatians* (1535), LW 27:13–14. "... recedunt a iusticia et vita longius quam Publicani, Peccatores et Meretrices. Illi enim non possunt niti fiducia operum suorum, cum talia sint, propter quae non possint confidere se consecuturos gratiam et remissionem peccatorum. ... Sunt igitur feliciores hac in parte iusticiariis, quia deest eis propriorum operum fiducia, quae si non penitus tollit fidem in Christum, tamen

maxime eam impedit. E contra Iusticiarii abstinentes externe a peccatis et in speciem inculpate et religiose viventes non possunt carere opinione fiduciae et iusticiae, cum qua stare non potest fides in Christum. Ideoque infeliciores sunt publicanis et meretricibus, qui Deo irato non offerunt sua bona opera, ut pro eis reddat ipsis vitam aeternam (ut Operarii), cum nulla habeant, sed ignosci sibi sua peccata propter Christum petunt etc." WA 40/2:15, 28—16, 17.

Chapter 4: Two Kinds of Love and the Worth of Creation

1. *Lectures on Galatians* (1535), LW 26:129. "Nos autem loco charitatis istius ponimus fidem." WA 40/1:228, 27.

2. See, e.g., Anders Nygren, *Eros och Agape*, 2:251–374 (English: *Agape and Eros*; trans. Philip S. Watson [London: SPCK, 1953]); Helmut Kuhn, *Liebe: Geschichte eines Begriffes* (Munich, 1975), 80–92.

3. Thomas à Kempis, *The Imitation of Christ*, Books 1–3, trans. Leo Sherley-Price (New York: Penguin Books, 1952), 114. "Expecta modicum, anima mea; expecta divinum promissum, et habebis abundantiam omnium bonorum in Coelo. Si nimis inordinate ista appetis praesentia, perdes aeterna et coelestia. Sint temporalia in usu, aeterna in desiderio. Non potes aliquo bono temporali satiari, quia ad haec fruenda non es creata." *De imitatione Christi libri quatuor* (sine nomine); ed. T. Lupio (Vatican City, 1982), 176, 4–7.

4. *The Imitation of Christ*, 167. "Fili, pretiosa est gratia mea; non patitur se misceri extraneis rebus nec consolationibus terrenis. Abicere ergo oportet omnia impedimenta gratiae, si optas eius infusionem suscipere. Pete secretum tibi; ama solus habitare tecum; nullius require confabulationem, sed magis ad Deum devotam effunde precem, ut compunctam teneas mentem et puram conscientiam. Totum mundum nihil aestima. Dei vacationem omnibus exterioribus antepone. Non enim poteris mihi vacare et in transitoriis pariter delectari. A notis et a caris oportet elongari et ab omni temporali solatio mentem tenere privatam." *De imitatione*, 274, 1—275, 7.

5. *The Imitation of Christ*, 148–49. "Si scires te perfecte annihilare atque ab omni creato amore evacuare, tunc deberem in te cum magna gratia emanare. Quando tu respicis ad creaturas, subtrahitur tibi aspectus Creatoris. Disce te in omnibus propter Creatorem vincere: tunc ad divinam valebis cognitionem pertingere. Quantumcumque modicum sit, si quid inordinate diligitur et respicitur, retardat a summo Bono et vitiat." *De imitatione*, 242, 9–12.

6. *The Imitation of Christ*, 135. "Oportet igitur omnem pertransire creaturam et se ipsum perfecte deserere ac in excessu mentis stare, et videre te omnium Conditorem cum creaturis nil simile habere. Et nisi quis ab omnibus creaturis fuerit expeditus, non poterit libere intendere divinis." *De imitatione*, 216, 5–6.

7. *The Imitation of Christ*, 98. "Nil dulcius est amore, nil fortius, nil altius, nil latius, nil iucundius, nil plenius, nil melius in coelo et in terra, quia amor a Deo natus est, nec potest nisi in Deo super omnia creata quiescere. Amans volat, currit, laetatur, liber est et non tenetur. Dat omnia pro omnibus et habet omnia in omnibus, quia in Uno summo super omnia quiescit, ex quo omne bonum fluit et procedit. Non respicit ad dona, sed ad donantem se convertit super omnia bona. Amor saepe modum nescit, sed super omne bonum fervescit. Amor onus non sentit, labores non reputat, plus affectat quam valet, de impossibilitate non causatur, quia cuncta sibi licet et posse arbitratur. Valet igitur ad omnia et multa implet et effectui mancipat." *De imitatione*, 216, 5–6.

8. *The Imitation of Christ*, 98–99. "Ubi vero amans deficit et iacet, amor vigilat, et dormiens non dormitat, fatigatus non laxatur, artatus non artatur, territus non conturbatur, sed sicut vivax flamma et ardens favilla sursum erumpit secureque pertransit. Si quis amat, novit quid haec vox clamat. Magnus clamor in auribus Dei est ardens

114 | Chapter 5 Notes

affectus animae, quae dicit: —Deus Deus meus, amor meus, tu totus meus et ego tuus. —Dilata me in amore, ut discam interiora cordis degustare, quam suave sit amare et in amore liquefieri et natare. Tenear amore, vadens supra me prae nimio favore et stupore. Cantem amoris canticum, sequar te Dilectum meum in altum. Deficit in laude tua anima mea iubilans ex amore. Amem te plus quam me, nec me nisi propter te, et omnes in te qui vere amant te, sicut iubet lex amoris lucens ex te." *De imitatione*, 146, 22—147, 29.

9. Martin Luther, The Large Catechism, in *The Book of Concord: The Confessions of the Evangelical Lutheran Church*; ed. Robert Kolb and Timothy Wengert (Minneapolis: Fortress Press, 2000), 432.

10. "Thus our hearts will be warmed and kindled with gratitude to God and a desire to use all these blessings to his glory and praise." Ibid., 433.

11. Heiko Oberman, *Luther: Man between God and the Devil*; trans. Eileen Walliser-Schwartzbart (New Haven & London: Yale University Press, 1989), 273–74 (German original: *Luther: Mensch zwischen Gott und Teufel* [Berlin, 1982]).

12. Oberman, *Luther*, 272. *Christliche Schrift, sich in den ehelichen Stand zu begeben* (1525), WA 18:277, 26–27.

13. Oberman, *Luther*, 275–76. *Wider den falsch genannten geistlichen Stand des Papstes und der Bischöfe,* WA 10/2:156, 16–22.

14. See Lauri Haikola, *Usus legis* (Uppsala: Lundequistska, 1958).

Chapter 5: Faith and God's Creative Love for "What Is Not" and for "Evil"

1. See *In Natali Christi* (Christmas Sermon) (1515), WA 1:20–25.

2. "Es weyßet auch wol ettwas hievon das menschlich wort; denn ynn demselben erkennet man des menschen hertz, alß man spricht gemeiniglich: Ich hab seyn hertz odder seyn meynung, ßo er doch nur seyn wort hatt, darumb das dem wortt des hertzen meynung folgt und durchs wortt erkennt wirtt, alsz were es ynn dem wort, daher die erfarung auch die hyden geleret hatt, das sie sprechen: Qualis quisque est, talia loquitur. Was eyner fur man ist, darnach redet er auch. Item: Oratio est character animi, die rede ist eyn ebenbild odder controfeytt bild des hertzen." *Kirchenpostille* (Church Postil) (1522), WA 10/1/1:187, 9–16. [Italics and brackets are added by the author.—Ed.]

3. "Ist seyn wortt yhm ßo ebengleych, das die gottheyt gantz drynnen ist, unnd wer das wortt hatt, der hatt die gantze gottheyt. Aber es feylet hie diß gleychniß auch; denn das menschlich wort bringt nit weßenlich oder die natur des hertzen mit sich, ßondernn nur bedeutlich, odder alß eyn tzeychen, wie das holtz-odder golltbild nit mit sich bringt das menschlich weßen, das es bedeuttet. Aber hie ynn gott bringt das wortt nit alleyn das tzeychen und bild, ßondernn auch das gantz weßen mit sich und ist ebenßo voller gott, alß der, des bild oder wort es ist. *Kirchenpostille*, WA 10/1/1:188, 7–17. [The translation is revised with respect to unnecessary masculine pronouns. —Ed.]

4. See, e.g., *Adventspostille* (Advent Postil) (1522), WA 10/1/2:167, 32—168, 16.

5. *In Natali Christi*, WA 1:28.

6. *Adventspostille*, WA 10/1/2:42, 5–12.

7. "Ibi caro nihil videt, concludit: Ex nihilo nihil fit, et tamen omnia futura videmus per verbum consolacionis in hoc Nihilo." *Vorlesung über Jesaias* (Lectures on Isaiah) (1527–1530), WA 31/2:363, 25–27.

8. *The Magnificat* (1521), LW 21:303–4; WA 7:551, 12–24.

9. *In Natali Christi*, WA 1:28.

10. *Crucigers Sommerpostille* (Cruciger's Summer Postil) (1544), WA 21:457, 11–28.

11. *The Freedom of a Christian* (1520), LW 31:345. "Animam posse omnibus rebus carere excepto verbo dei, sine quo nullis prorsus rebus est illi consultum. Habens autem verbum dives est, nullius egens, cum sit verbum vitae, veritatis, lucis, pacis, iustitiae, salutis, gaudii, libertatis, sapientiae, virtutis, gratiae, gloriae et omnis boni inaestimabiliter." WA 7:50, 39—51, 3.

12. *The Freedom of a Christian*, LW 31:346. "Neque enim verbum dei operibus ullis, sed sola fide suscipi et coli potest. Ideo clarum est, ut solo verbo anima opus habet ad vitam et iustitiam, ita sola fide et nullis operibus iustificatur." WA 7: 51, 20–23.

13. *Lectures on Galatians* (1535), LW 26:129–30. "Nos autem loco charitatis istius ponimus fidem. . . . Sed si est vera fides, est quaedam certa fiducia cordis et firmus assensus quo Christus apprehenditur, Sic ut Christus sit obiectum fidei, imo non obiectum, sed, ut ita dicam, in ipsa fide Christus adest. Fides ergo est cognitio quaedam vel tenebra quae nihil videt, Et tamen in istis tenebris Christus fide apprehensus sedet, Quemadmodum Deus in Sinai et in Templo sedebat in medio tenebrarum. Est ergo formalis nostra iustitia non charitas informans fidem, sed ipsa fides et nebula cordis, hoc est, fiducia in rem quam non videmus, hoc est, in Christum qui, ut maxime non videatur, tamen praesens est. Iustificat ergo fides, quia apprehendit et possidet istum thesaurum, scilicet Christum praesentem. Sed quo modo praesens sit, non est cogitabile, quia sunt tenebrae, ut dixi. Ubi ergo vera fiducia cordis est, ibi adest Christus in ipsa nebula et fide. Eaque est formalis iustitia propter quam homo iustificatur, non propter charitatem, ut Sophistae loquuntur. Summa: Sicut Sophistae dicunt charitatem formare et imbuere fidem, Sic nos dicimus Christum formare et imbuere fidem vel formam esse fidei. Ergo fide apprehensus et in corde habitans Christus est iustitia Christiana propter quam Deus nos reputat iustos et donat vitam aeternam. Ibi certe nullum est opus legis, nulla dilectio, sed longe alia iustitia et novus quidam mundus extra et supra legem; Christus enim vel fides non est Lex nec opus legis." WA 40/1:228, 27—229, 32.

14. "Und du keyn ander werck fur yhm thun, denn solchs glawbenn, das Christus seyne werck fur dich thu unnd setze gegen gott, auff das alßo deyn glawbe lautter bleyb, nichts thue, denn hallte stille, laß yhm wolthun und empfahe Christus werck, und lasse Christus seyne liebe an yhm uben. Du must blind, lahm, tawb, todt, außsetzig und arm seyn, odder wirst dich an Christo ergernn. Das Euangelion leugt dyr nicht, das Christum nur unter solchen durfftigen lesst sehen und wolthun." *Adventspostille*, WA 10/1/2:168, 5–11.

15. "Ita nec nos qui sumus caro sic efficimur verbum, quod in verbum substantialiter mutemur, sed quod assumimus et per fidem ipsum nobis unimus, qua unione non tantum habere verbum sed etiam esse dicimur." *In Natali Christi*, WA 1:28, 39–41.

16. *The Freedom of a Christian*, LW 31:367. "Dabo itaque me quendam Christum proximo meo, quemadmodum Christus sese praebuit mihi." WA 7:66, 3–4.

17. *The Freedom of a Christian*, LW 31:367–68. "Ideo sicut pater coelestis nobis in Christo gratis auxiliatus est, ita et nos debemus gratis per corpus et opera eius proximo nostro auxiliari et unusquisque alteri Christus quidam fieri, ut simus mutuum Christi et Christus idem in omnibus, hoc est, vere Christiani." WA 7:66, 25–28.

18. *On Christian Freedom* (1520), LW 31:368. "Hodie in toto orbe ignota est, . . . adeo ut prorsus nostrum nomen ipsimet ignoremus, cur Christiani simus et vocemur. certe a Christo sic vocamur, non absente sed inhabitante in nobis, idest, dum credimus in eum, et invicem mutuoque sumus alter alterius Christus facientes proximis, sicut Christus nobis facit." WA 7:66, 32–36.

19. "Erfinden teglich ßo viel newer werck und lere, das wyr tzuletzt nichts mehr wissen vonn rechtem gutem leben, ßo doch alle Christlich lere, werck und leben kurtz, klarlich, ubirflussig begriffen ist ynn den zweyen stucken GLAWBEN UND LIEBEN, durch

wilch der mensch tzwischen Gott unnd seynem nehisten gesetzt wirt alß eyn mittell, das da von oben empfehet und unten widder außgibt unnd gleych eyn gefeß oder rhor wirt durch wilchs der brun gotlicher gutter on unterlas fließen soll ynn andere leutt. Sihe, das sind denn recht gottformige menschen, wilche von gott empfahen allis, was er hatt, ynn Christo, und widderumb sich auch, alß weren sie der andern gotte, mit wolthaten beweißen; da geht denn der spruch ps. 81 (82,6): Ich hab gesagt, yhr seyt Gotter und kinder des allerhochsten allesampt. Gottis kinder sind wyr durch den glawben, der unß erben macht aller gottlichen gutter. Aber gotte synd wyr durch die liebe, die unß gegen unßernn nehisten wolthettig macht; denn gottlich natur ist nit anderß denn eytell wolthettickeyt und, alß hie S. Paulus sagt, freundlickeit und leutselickeyt, die yhr gutter ynn alle creatur ubirschwenglich außschuttet teglich, wie wyr sehen." *Kirchenpostille*, WA 10/1/1:100, 7—101, 2. [Translated by the author and the translator.—Ed.]

Chapter 6: Christians as "Christs" to Their Neighbors

1. "Alle andere werck außer dem glawben sollen wyr auff den nehisten richten, denn gott foddert von uns keyn werck an yhn tzu thun, denn alleyn denn glawben durch Christum; daran hatt er gnug, damit geben wyr yhm seyne ehre als dem, der gnedig, barmhertzig, weyß, gutt, warhafftig ist und desgleychen. Darnach denck nicht mehr, denn: thu dem nehisten, wir dyr Christus than hatt, und laß alle deyne werck mitt gantzem leben auff deynen nehisten gericht seyn. Suche, wo arme, krancken und allerley geprechliche sind, den hilff, da laß deynes leben ubung stehen, das sie deyner geniessen, wer deyn darff, ßo viel du vormagist, mit leyb, gutt, und ehre." *Adventspostille* (Advent Postil) (1522), WA 10/1/2:168, 18–26. [Translated by the author and the translator.—Ed.]

2. "Die liebe aber ist das heubt, der brunn und gemeyne tugent aller tugent. Liebe speyset, trencket, kleydet, tröstet, bittet, löset, hilfft und redt. Was soll man sagen? Sihe ergibt sich selb mit leyb und leben, mit guet und ehre, mit allen krefften ynnwendig und auswendig zur not und nutz des nehisten, beyde feyndes und freundes, behellt nichts, damit sie nicht diene dem andern. Darumb ist yhr keyne tugent zu gleichen, und mag auch yhr keyn eygen sonderlich werck ausgemalet odder genennet werden, wie man den andern stucklichen tugenten thuet, als da sind keuscheyt, barmhertzickeyt, geduld, sanfftmut usw. Die liebe thut allerley und. . ., das wol S. Paulus hie sagt: 'Alle gepot sind ynn dem wort verfasset alls ynn eyner summa 'Liebe deynen nehisten.'" *Fastenpostille* (Lenten Postil) (1525), WA 17/2:100, 26—101, 4. [Translated by the author and the translator. Words such as *"guet"* and *"thuet"* are rendered with letters available in English.—Ed.]

3. "So ist nu dis gepot der liebe Eyn kurtz gepot und lang gepott, Eyn eynig gepot und viel gepot. Es ist keyn gepot und alle gepot, kurtz und eynig ists an yhm selbs und des verstands halben bald gefasst. Aber lang und viel nach der ubunge, denn es begrryfft und meystert alle gepot. Und ist gar keyn gepot, so man die werck ansihet. Denn es hat keyn eygen sonder werck mit namen. Aber es ist alle gepot, darumb, das aller gepot werck seyne werck sind und seyn sollen. Also hebt der liebe gepot auff alle gepot und setzt doch alle gepot auff." *Fastenpostille*, WA 17/2:95, 17–21.

4. "Man hatt also viel bucher und lere gegeben, der menschen leben zu unterrichten, das derselben widder zal noch ende ist, und ist noch keyn auffhoren, bucher und gesetz zu machen, wie wyr sehen ynn geystlichen und welltlichen rechten. . . . Und were das alles noch zu leyden und eyn sondere gnade, wo solch gesetz und lere alle wurden gezogen und gehandellt nach dem heubtgesetz, regel und mas der liebe, wie die heylige schrifft thut, wilche auch viel und mancherley gesetz gibt, aber allesampt ynn die liebe zeucht und fasset, der liebe auch die selbe alle unterwirfft. Also das sie alle mussen

weychen und nymmer gesetz seyn noch ettwas gellten, wo es die liebe trifft." *Fastenpostille*, WA 17/2:91, 7–16. [Translated by the author and the translator.—Ed.]

5. *Lectures on Galatians* (1535), LW 27:57–58. "Breve verbum est et pulchre ac potenter dictum: 'Diliges proximum tuum sicut Teipsum.' Nemo potest dare melius, certius et propius exemplum quam Seipsum. Neque dari potest nobilior et profundior habitus quam charitas, Neque excellentius obiectum quam proximus. Exemplum ergo, habitus et obiectum sunt nobilissima. Itaque si cupis scire, quo modo diligendus sit proximus, et habere exemplum illustre huius rei, considera diligenter, quo modo Tu teipsum diligas. Certe cuperes anxie in necessitate aut periculo te amari et iuvari omnibus consiliis, facultatibus et viribus non solum omnium hominum sed etiam omnium creaturarum. Quare nullo libro indiges, qui te erudiat et admoneat, quomodo proximum diligere debeas, habes enim pulcherrimum et optimum librum omnium legum in corde tuo. Non egis ullo doctore hac in re, tantum consule tuum proprium cor, hoc satis abunde docebit te, ita diligendum esse tuum proximum, ut Teipsum. Deinde charitas summa virtus est, quae non solum parata est servire lingua, manu pecunia, facultatibus, sed etiam corpore et ipsa vita." WA 40/2:72, 14–28.

6. *Lectures on Romans*, LW 25:475. "Quia per hoc verbum 'Sicut teipsum' excluditur omnis Simulatio dilectionis. Vnde Qui diligit proximum Vel propter diuitias, gloriam, eruditionem, fauorem, potentiam, consolationem, et non itidem, qui est pauper, ignobilis, indoctus, aduersarius, subiectus, asper, patet, Quod simulate diligit, Non ipsum, Sed ea, que sunt illius, ad suam comoditatem, Ac per hoc non 'vt seipsum', Quippe qui seipsum diligit, etiamsi sit pauper, insulsus et penitus nihil. Quis enim tam inutilis, qui sese odiat? Et tamen Nullus tam nihil, Quin seipsum diligat et alios non ita diligat. Ideo istud preceptum arduissimum est, si recte ruminetur." WA 56:482, 29—483, 11.

7. *Lectures on Romans* (1515–1516), LW 25:476. "Diuites tezaurisant sacerdotes pro edificio Ecclesiarum Vel memoriis. Si autem induerent affectum pauperis Et secum disputarent, An etiam sibi vellent non donari, Sed potius Ecclesiis, facile quid facere deberent, ex seipsis scirent." WA 56:483, 21–24.

8. "Und damit verwirfft S. Paulus der Sophisten trewme, die von der liebe also reden, das sie von eynander scheyden die eusserliche werck und die ynnerliche gunst und sprechen, die liebe seyn eyn ynnerliche gunst und habe den nehisten lieb, wenn sie yhm ynnerlich guts gonnet. . . . Das las faren. Hie sihestu, das S. Paulus liebe heyst nicht gunst allein, sondern gunstige wolthat." *Fastenpostille*, WA 17/2:98, 28–33. [Translated by the author and the translator.]

9. "Er spricht nicht: Du sollt lieben den reichen, gewelltigen, gelerten, heyligen. . . . Sondern da ist keyn ansehen der person. Denn das thuet die falsche, fleyschliche wellt liebe, die alleyne sihet auff die person und liebet, so lange sie nutz und hoffnung hat. Wo nutz und hoffnung aus ist, ist die liebe auch aus. Aber diss gepott foddert die freye liebe gegen yderman, unangesehen, wer er ist, er sey feynd odder freund. Denn sie sucht nicht nutz noch gut, sondern sie gibt und thuet nutz und gut. Darumb ist sie am thettigesten und mechtigesten gegen die armen, durftigen, boesen, sundern, narren, krancken und feynden. Denn da findet sie zu dulden, leyden, tragen, dienen und wolzuthuen alle hende vol. . . ." *Fastenpostille*, WA 17/2:101, 6–17. [Words such as "*boesen*," "*sundern*," and "*thuet*" are rendered with letters available in English. Translated by the author and the translator.—Ed.]

10. "Nu das eüßerlich werck der liebe ist ser groß, wenn wir unser gut lassen dem anderen ein knecht werden. Aber das groest ist das, wenn ich mein gerechtigkeit hyn gib und dienen laß des nechsten sünde. Dann mit dem gut eüsserlich dienen und helffen, ist die liebe allein. Aber die gerechtigkeit dar zustrecken, disß ist groß, do musß ich im frid sein und lieb haben. . . . so lieb soll ich jn haben, das ich jm auch nochlauff und werd wie der hyrrt der das schaff sucht unnd die fraw die den verlornen pfennig sucht.

Darumb woellen wir hye reden von dem hohen werck der liebe, das ein frumm mann sein gerechtigkeit setz für den sünder, ein frumm weyb ir eer für die ergsten huren. Das thut nu die welt und vernunfft nit. Dann wo allein vernunfft ist und redlich frumm leüt seind, die vermügen solichs nit zu thun, sonder woellen ir frommkeit allein damit beweißen, das sye die nasen künnen rümpffen gegen den sünderen." *Predigt* (Sermon) (1522), WA 10/3:217, 13–30. [Translated by the author and the translator. Words such as "*groest*" and "*woellen*" are rendered with letters available in English.—Ed.]

11. "Und das seind die rechten christlichen werck, das man hynfall, wickel und flick sich in des sünders schlam so tieff als er drinn steckt, und nem des sünd uff sich und wuel sich mit heruß und thu nit anders dann als weren sye sein eygen." *Predigt*, WA 10/3:218, 26–29. [Translated by the author and the translator.—Ed.]

12. *The Freedom of a Christian* (1520), LW 31:371. "En, ista regula oportet, ut quae ex deo habemus bona fluant ex uno in alium et comunia fiant, ut unus quisque proximum suum induat et erga eum sic se gerat, ac si ipse esset in Loco illius. E Christo fluxerunt in nos, qui nos sic induit et pro nobis egit, ac si ipse esset quod nos sumus. E nobis fluunt in eos, qui eis opus habent, adeo ut et fidem et iustitiam meam oporteat coram deo poni pro tegendis et deprecandis proximi peccatis, quae super me accipiam, et ita in eis laborem et serviam, ac si mea propria essent: sic enim Christus nobis fecit. Haec est enim vera charitas synceraque Christianae vitae regula." WA 7:69, 1–9.

13. "Mit dem eynigen wort verdampt S. Paulus aller heuchel heyligen wesen und regiment. Denn der selben wesen steht also, das sie mit sundern und geprechlichen nicht kunden umbgehen. Es mues alles nach der strenge yhrer gesetz gehen. Da ist eyttel treyben und iagen, keyne barmhertzickeyt, sondern eyttel straffen, schelten, urteylen, taddeln und toben. Nichts unrechts mugen sie leyden. Aber bey den Christen steht es also, das sie viel sunder und gebrechlichen bey sich haben, ia alleyne mit den selben umbgehen und nicht mit den heyligen. Darumb verwerffen sie niemand, tragen ydermann, ia, sie nemen sich der selben so hertzlich an, als weren sie selbs ynn solchem geprechen, beten fur sie und leren, vermanen und reytzen sie und thun alles, was sie muegen, damit sie den selben helffen. Das ist eyn rechte Christliche art, so hatt uns Gott ynn Christo than und thuet noch stets also." *Fastenpostille*, WA 17/2:111, 32—112, 10. [Translated by the author and the translator. Words such as "*mues*" and "*muegen*" are rendered with letters available in English.—Ed.]

14. "So ist nu das die Summa des Euangelions, Das reich Christi ist ein reich der barmhertzikeit und Gnad, da nichts anders ist dann ymmer tragenn und tragen. Christus treget unsere gebrechen und kranckheytten, unser sünde nimpt er auf sich und hat gedult, wann wir feelen, wir ligen ime noch ymmerdar auff dem halße, und er würt des tragens nit mued. Die Prediger inn disem reich sollen die gewissen troesten, sollenn freündtlich mit jnen umbgeen, sollen sie speysen mit dem Euangelio, sollenn dy schwachenn tragen, die kranckenn heylen. . . . und einem yegklichen, nach dem es ym von noeten, fürtragen.

"Das ist das ampt eines rechten Bischoff und predigers, unnd nit mit gewalt faren, wie unsere bischoff yetzt thun, die da stoecken und bloecken und schreyen: huy hinan hinan, wer nicht wil, der muß. Nicht also, Sonder ein Bischoff unnd Prediger sol sich stellen wie einer, der der krancken wartet, der get gar seüberlich mit jn umb, gibt gute wort, redet fein freündtlich mit den krancken unt thut allen vleyß bey jn. Also sol ein Bischoffe unnd Pfarrer auch thun, und sol nicht anders gedencken, denn das sein Bistumb und Pfarre ein Spital und siechhauß sey, darinne er gar vil und mancherley krankken habe." *Sommerpostille* (Summer Postil) (1526), WA 10/1/2:366, 18–34. [Translated by the author and the translator. Words such as "*stoeken*" and "*bloecken*" are rendered with letters available in English.—Ed.]

15. "Also geet es under uns auch, das wir all ein kuchen werden eynander essen. Ir
wißt, wenn man brot machet, so zureybt man und zumalt alle korner, so wirt den yeglich korn des andern korns mel, wirt also undereynander gemenget, das man ynn eym
sack voll mel, wie die kornlin so ynn eynander gestossen synd, das yeglichs des andern
mel ist worden, und behelt keyns sein gestalt, sundern gibt yhe eyns dem andern seyn
mel unnd verlieret yeglichs seyn leyb, also das viler kornlin leybe eyns brots leybe werden; desselben gleychen, wen man weyn machet, menget yeglich weynberlin sein safft
ynn der ander ber safft, und verlieret yeglichs seyn gestalt, das also eyn tranck draus
wirt. Also soll es mit uns auch seyn, wenn ich mich gemeyn mache unnd diene dir, das
du meyn geneussest, wazu du meyn bedarffst, so byn ich dein speyß, Eben als du des
brots geneussest, wen du hungerig bist, das deym leib und dem hungerigen magen hilfft
unnd krafft gibt. Darumb wen ich dir ynn aller not hilffe und diene, so bin ich auch dein
brot, Widerumb bystu auch ein Christ, so thust du auch wider also, das du mit allem,
was du hast, mir dienest, das mirs alles zu gut kompt unnd ich des selben geniesse wie
der speyße oder des trancks; Ists, das ich eyn sünder byn und du von Gottis gnaden
frum bist, so farstu zu, unnd teylist mir deyn frumket mit, bittest fur mich, tritst fur
mich fur Got unnd nymest dich mein also an, alls werstus selbs, also verzerestu mit
deiner frumket meine sünd, wie Christus uns thon hat, also yssestu mich, so yss ich dich
wider." *Predigt* (Sermon) (1523), WA 12:489, 9—490, 5. [Translation and bracketed text
are by the author and the translator.—Ed.]

Chapter 7: Love for God

1. See above, chap. 4, "Two Kinds of Love and the Worth of Creation."
2. For no good reason, discussion of Nygren's thesis has remained scarce. One reason
for this may be Nygren's use of the concepts *eros* and *agape*, a decision that cannot be
considered successful.
3. *The Magnificat* (1521), LW 21:300. "Darumb bleibt got allein solchs ansehen, das
ynn die tieffe not vnd iamer sihet, vnd ist nah allen den, die ynn der tieffe sein. Vnd
als Petrus sagt: den hohen widdersteet er, den nidrigen gibt er seine gnade. Und ausz
dieszem grund fleusset nu die lieb unnd das lob gottis. Es mag yhe niemant got loben,
er hab ihn dann zuvor lieb, szo mag yhn niemant lieben, er sey ym dann auffs lieblichst
und aller best bekant. Szo mag er nit alszo bekant werden denn durch seine werck ynn
unsz erzeygt, gefuelet unnd erfaren: wo aber erfarenn wirt, wie er ein solcher got ist, der
ynn die tieffe sihett, vnd nur hilfft den armen, vorachten, elendenn, iamerichen, vorlas-
senen, vnnd die gar nichts seint, da wirt er szo hertzlich lieb, da geht das hertzuber fur
freudenn, hupfft und springet fur grossem wolgefallen, den es ynn got empfangen." *Sta*
1:318, 11–21; WA 7:547, 33—548, 10. [The translation is revised with respect to unnecessary masculine pronouns.—Ed.]
4. *The Magnificat*, LW 21:302. "Alszo gahn gottes werck und gesicht ynn der tieffe,
menschen gesicht vnd werck nur ynn der hohe. Das ist nu die ursach yhrs lobszangs. . .
." *Sta* 1:319, 29–31; WA 7:549, 29–31. [Translation revised.—Ed.]
5. *The Magnificat*, LW 21:317. "Kurtzlich : Es leret vnsz dieszer versz recht gott
erkennenn, unnd inn dem das er antzeygt. Got sehe auff die nydrigenn, vorachten. Und der
erkent got recht, der so weysz das got auff die nydrigen sihet, . . . und ausz dem erkent-
nisz folget denn lieb unnd traw zu got, das sich der mensch yhm willig ergibt vnd folget."
Sta 1:332, 29–33; WA 7:564, 18–22.
6. Cf., e.g., *The Magnificat*, LW 21:307; *Sta* 1:323, 36; WA 7:554, 7–9.
7. Heidelberg Disputation (1518), LW 31:56–57; *Sta* 1:211, 15–25; *Sta* 1:212, 8–9;
WA 1:364, 28–38; WA 1:365, 8–10.
8. *The Magnificat*, LW 21:302. "Es schwebt meinn leben unnd alle mein synn ynn
gottis lieb, lob vnd hohen freuden, das ich mein selb nit mechtig, mehr erhaben werde,
denn mich selb erhebe zu gottis lob, wie denn geschicht allen denen, die mit gotlicher

sussickeit vnd geyst durchgossen werden, das sie mehr fuelen, denn sie sagen kundenn. Denn es ist kein menschen werck, got mit frewden lobenn. Es ist mehr ein frolich leyden, vnd allein ein gottis werck, das sich mit worten nit leren / szondernn nur durch eigenn erfarung kennen lessit." *Sta* 1:319, 36—320, 2; WA 7:550, 5–11.

9. *The Magnificat*, LW 21:309. "Damit sie unsz leret, wie wir sollen got blosz und recht ordenlich lieben und loben, und ia nichts das unszer an ihm suchen, der liebt aber vnd lobet blosz vnd recht got, der ihn nur darumb lobet, daß er gut ist, und nit mehr denn seine blosze gutickeyt ansihet, und nur ynn der selben sein lust und freude hat, wilchs ist ein hohe reine zarte weisze zu lieben und loben, die wol eigent einem solchen hohen zarten geist, alsz diszer iunckfrawen ist. Die unreinen und vorkereten liebhaber, wilche nit lieben nit denn lautter nieszlinge sein, und das yhre an got suchenn, die lieben und loben nit seine blosze gutickeit, sondernn sehen auff sich selb, und achten nur, wie viel got uber sie gut sey. . . ." *Sta* 1:326, 4–13; WA 7:556, 18–29. [Translation revised with respect to unnecessary masculine pronouns.—Ed.]

10. *The Magnificat*, LW 21:309–10. "Wenn sich aber got vorpirget, und seiner gutheit glentze zu sich zeugt, das sie blosz und elend sein, szo gaht auch lieb und lob zu gleich ausz, und mugen nit die blosze unempfindliche gutte, ynn got vorporgen, lieben noch loben, damit sie beweissen, das nit yhr geyst sich ynn got dem heyland erfrewet hat, ist nit rechte lieb und lob der blossen gutte da geweszen, szondernn viel mehr haben sie lust gehabt ynn dem heyl, denn ym heyland, mehr ynn den gaben, denn ynn dem geber, mehr ynn der Creaturn denn ynn got. Denn sie kunnen nit gleich bleiben, ynn haben und mangellnn, ynn reichtumb und armut, wie Sankt Paulus sagt: Ich hab erlernet, das ich kan uberig haben, und mangel habenn." *Sta* 1:326, 16–25; WA 7:556, 30—557, 5. [Translation revised with respect to unnecessary masculine pronouns.—Ed.]

11. *The Magnificat*, LW 21:311. "Warlich ists eyn geyst, der nur ym glawben da er springt, und hupfft nit von den gutternn gottis, die sie empfand, szondernn nur von got, den sie nit empfand, frolich ist, als von yhrem heyl, den sie nur ym glawben erkennet. O das seind die rechten, nydrigen, ledigen, hungerigen, gotfurchtigen geyste. . . ." *Sta* 1:327, 39—328, 1; WA 7:558, 25–29.

12. "Ob nu wol der glaube das gesetze nicht fuellet, so hat er doch das, damit es erfuellet wird, denn er erwirbet den geyst und die liebe, damit es erfullet wird. Widderumb, ob die liebe nicht rechtfertiget, so beweyset sie doch das, damit die person rechtfertig ist, nemlich den glauben. Und summa, wie hie S. Paulus selbs davon redet: 'Die liebe ist des gesetzs erfullung', als sollt er sagen: Es ist eyn ander rede, des gesetzs erfuellung seyn und des gesetzs erfuellung machen odder geben. Die liebe erfuellet also das gesetz, das sie selbs die erfuellung ist. Aber der glaub erfuellet also das gesetze, das er darreicht, da mit es erfuellet wird. Denn der glaub liebet und wirckt, wie Gal. 5. sagt: 'Der glaub ist thettig durch die liebe.' Das wasser fuellet den krug, der schenck fuellet auch den krug, das wasser durch sich selbs, der schenck durchs wasser. Das hiessen die Sophisten auff yhre sprach Effective et formaliter implere." *Fastenpostille* (Lenten Postil) (1525), WA 17/2:98, 13–24.

13. "Wir erfullet werden auff alle weise, damit er voll macht und voll Gotes werden uberschuttet mit allen gaben und gnade und erfullet mit seynem geyst, der uns mutig mache und mit seynem liecht erleucht und seyn leben ynn uns lebe, seyne selickeit uns selig mache, seyne liebe yn uns die liebe erwecke." *Predigt* (Sermon) October 1, 1525; WA 17/1:438, 15–19. [Translated by the author and the translator.—Ed.]

14. *Treatise on Good Works* (1520), LW 44:26–28. "Wen ein man odder weib sich zum andern vorsicht lieb vnd wolgefallens, vnd das selb fest glewbt, wer lernet den selben wie er sich stellen sol, was er thun, lassen, sagen, schweigen, gedencken sol? die eynige zuworsicht leret yhn das alles und mehr dan not ist. Da ist yhm kein vnterscheidt in wercken. Thut das grosz, lang, viele, szo gerne, als das klein, kurtz, wenige,

vnd widerumb, dartzu, mit frolichem, fridlichem, sicherem hertzen, vnd ist gantz ein frey geselle. Wo aber ein tzweifel da ist, da sucht sichs, welchs am bestenn sey, da hebet sich unterscheidt der werck austzumalen, wamit er mug huld erwerben, vnd gaht den-noch zu mit schwerem hertzen vnd grosem unlust, unnd ist gleich gefangen, mehr dan halb vortzweiffelt, und wirt offt zum narren drob. Alszo einn Christen mensch, der in diser zuuorsicht gegen got lebt, weisz alle ding, vormag alle dingk, vormisset sich aller ding, was zu thun ist, und thuts alles frolich und frey, nit vmb vil guter vordinst unnd werck zusamlen, szondern das yhm eine lust ist, got alszo wolgefallen, vnd leuterlich umb sunst got dienet, daran benuget, das es got gefellet. Widderumb der mit got nit einz ist odder tzweyffelt darn, der hebt an, sucht vnd sorget, wie er doch wolle gnugthun und mit vil wercken got bewegen. Er . . . findet nit ruge, vnd thut das alles mit grosser beschwerung, vortzweyfflung, unnd unlust seines hertzen, das auch die schrifft solch gute werck nennet auff hebreisch Auen amal, auff deutsch, "muhe vnd erbeit," Dartzu seinsz nit gute werck vnd alle vorloren. . . . Von den steht Sap. v. wir sein muhd worden in dem unrechten wege und habenn schwere sawer wege gewandelt, aber gottis weg habe wir nit erkennet, und die son der gerechtickeit ist unsz nit auffgangen." *Sta* 2:20, 35—21, 25; WA 6:207, 16—208, 5. [Androcentric translations occur throughout LW; e.g., "Christen mensch" does not need to be translated as "Christian man"; the Finnish translation would be naturally gender inclusive, "kristitty ihminen." —Ed.]

15. *The Magnificat*, LW 21:334–36, esp. 336; *Sta* 1:346, 14–30; *Sta* 1:347, 18–31; WA 7:581, 6–18; 582, 15–29.

16. *The Magnificat*, LW 21:335–36. "Nu sihe wie hie die warheit wirt nit vorleugnet / die warheit sagt / es sein gutte ding vnd gottis creatur. Ja eben die selbe warheit / sagt auch vnd leret / dw solt solch gutte ding faren lassen / vnd alle stund bereyt sein yhr zuemperen / szo es got haben wil / vnd allein an got hangenn. Die warheit dringt dich nit / das du die gutter solt wider holen / damit das sie sagt / sie sein gut / dringt dich auch nit / das du solt sagen / sie sein nit gut / szondern das du solt der selben gelassen stehen / vnd bekennen das sie gut sind vnd nit bosze. [The translation is revised with respect to unnecessary masculine pronouns. —Ed.]

"Alszo musz man auch thun mit dem recht vnd allerley gutter der vornunfft odder weyszheit. Recht ist ein gut ding vnnd gabe gottis / wer zweyffelt daran? Gottis wort spricht selb / Recht sey gut / vnd sol yhe niemant bekennen das sein gutte odder rechte sach vnrecht odder bosze sey / sol ehe druber sterben / vnd allis was got nit ist / faren lassen / denn das were got vnnd sein wort vorleugket / der do sagt / recht sey gut vnd nit bosze. woltistu aber darumb schreyen / wutten / toben / vnnd alle welt erwurgen / das dyr solch recht wurd genummen / odder vordruckt? Als etlich thun die in den hymel ruffen / alle iamer anrichten / land vnd leut vorterben / mit kriegen vnd blut vorgissen die welt erfullen. Was weystu ob got dyr solche gabe vnnd recht lassen wil? Ists doch sein / mag dyrsz nehmen heut vnd morgen / drausz vnd drynnen / durch feynd vnd freund / vnnd wie er wil. Er vorsucht dich ob du auch vmb seinen willenn wollist des rechten emperen / vnrecht habe vnd leyden / vmb seynen willen die schande tragen / vnd an yhm allein hangenn. Bistu nw gotfurchtig / vnd denckist / herr / es ist deyn / ich wils nit haben / ich wisse denn das du myrsz gonnen wilt / far was da feret / sey du nur mein got." *Sta* 1:346, 36—347, 15; WA 7:581, 24—582, 12.

Afterword

1. This afterword is a substantially abbreviated and edited translation of Juhani Forsberg's "Die finnische Lutherforschung seit 1979," published in German in *Luther-Jahrbuch* 2005, 147–82. For the fuller text, consult the original article. For broader history on the Luther research in Finland, in German, see Miikka Ruokanen, ed., *Der Einfluss der Theologie Martin Luthers in Finnland und finnische Beiträge zur Lutherforschung*;

2nd ed. (Helsinki, 1986) and Eeva Martikainen, "Die finnische Lutherforschung seit 1934," in *ThR* 53 (1988), 371–87.

2. For some of the most important collections, see Tuomo Mannermaa, Anja Ghiselli, and Simo Peura, eds., *Thesaurus Lutheri: Auf der Suche nach neuen Paradigmen der Luther-Forschung* (Helsinki, 1987); Simo Peura and Antti Raunio, eds., *Luther und Theosis: Vergöttlichung als Thema der abendländischen Theologie* (Helsinki und Erlangen, 1990); Anja Ghiselli, Kari Kopperi, and Rainer Vinke, eds., *Luther und Ontologie: Das Sein Christi im Glauben als strukturierendes Prinzip der Theologie Luthers* (Helsinki und Erlangen 1993; Carl E. Braaten and Robert W. Jenson, eds., *Union with Christ: The New Finnish Interpretation of Luther* (Grand Rapids and Cambridge, 1998). Since 1991, the Nordische Forum für das Studium von Luther und lutherischer Theologie has published its presentations in the following collections: Tuomo Mannermaa, Petri Järveläinen, and Kari Kopperi, eds., *Nordiskt Forum för Studiet av Luther och luthersk teologi* 1 (Helsinki, 1993); Kari Kopperi, ed., *Widerspruch: Luthers Auseinandersetzung mit Erasmus von Rotterdam* (Helsinki, 1997); Ulrik Nissen, Anna Vind, Bo Holm, and Olli-Pekka Vainio, eds., *Luther between Present and Past: Studies in Luther and Lutheranism* (Helsinki, 2004). Other publications have come from the Luther-Akademie Ratzeburg and Martin-Luther-Bundes Erlangen: Joachim Heubach, ed., *Luther und die trinitarische Tradition: Ökumenische und trinitarische Perspektiven* (Ratzeburg und Erlangen, 1994); Joachim Heubach, ed., *Der Heilige Geist: Ökumenische und reformatorische Untersuchungen* (Ratzeburg und Erlangen, 1996).

3. For a comprehensive and up-to-date listing of the newest Finnish works on Luther and also international perspectives, see the "Finnish Luther Studies" website created by Risto Saarinen (University of Helsinki), www.helsinki.fi. For an overview of the international reception and critique of the Finnish Luther research, see also Risto Saarinen, "Die Teilhabe an Gott bei Luther und in der finnischen Lutherforschung," in *Luther und Ontologie*, 167–82.

4. The 1979 original Finnish work was published in English as *Christ Present in Faith: Luther's View of Justification* (Minneapolis: Fortress Press, 2005). In the preface, the editor Kirsi Stjerna interprets what Mannermaa means with the term "real ontic," or "Real-Ontischen," and warns against misinterpretations and misuses of the term. Mannermaa's later work on two kinds of love is now published in this volume.

5. Saarinen, "Die Teilhabe," 170.

6. Since 1980 about ten doctoral students of Mannermaa's have completed their dissertations on Luther's theology; his influence has been evident also in several other works with different foci and areas of concentration. [This number may already have increased.—Ed.]

7. Juhani Forsberg, *Das Abrahambild in der Theologie Luthers: Pater fidei sanctissimus* (Stuttgart, 1984).

8. Eero Huovinen, *Kuolemattomuudesta osallinen: Martti Lutherin kuoleman teologian ekumeeninen perusongelma* (Helsinki, 1981) (Participantion in Immortality: Martin Luther's Theology of Death and Its Central Ecumenical Problem); Huovinen, *Fides infantium: Martin Luthers Lehre vom Kinderglauben* (Mainz, 1997).

9. Risto Saarinen, *Gottes Wirken auf uns: Die transzendentale Deutung des Gegenwart-Christi-Motivs in der Lutherforschung* (Wiesbaden, 1989). Also Saarinen, "Gottes Sein—Gottes Wirken: Die Grunddifferenz von Substanzdenken und Wirkungsdenken in der evangelischen Lutherdeutung," in *Luther und Theosis*, 103–19.

10. Simo Peura, *Mehr als ein Mensch? Die Vergöttlichung als Thema der Theologie Martin Luthers von 1513 bis 1519* (Mainz, 1994). For more works on Peura, see Saarinen's "Finnish Luther Studies" website.

11. See, Peura, "Die Teilhabe," in *Luther und Theosis*, 121.

12. Antti Raunio, *Summe des christlichen Lebens: Die "Goldene Regel" als Gesetz der Liebe in der Theologie Martin Luthers von 1510—1527* (Mainz, 2001). For more articles from Raunio (e.g., on law and love), see Saarinen's "Finnish Luther Studies" website.

13. Jorma Laulaja, "Kultaisen säännön etiikka: Lutherin sosiaalietiikan luonnonoikeudellinen perusstruktuuri (Zusammenfassung: Die Ethik der Goldenen Regel: Die naturrechtliche Grundstruktur von Luthers Sozialethik)" (diss., Helsinki, 1981) (The Ethics of the golden rule: The Natural-Rights Basic Structure of Luther's Social Ethics).

14. Sammeli Juntunen, "Der Begriff des Nichts bei Luther in den Jahren von 1510 bis 1523" (diss., Helsinki, 1996).

15. Kari Kopperi, "Paradoksien teologia: Lutherin disputaatio Heidelbergissä 1518" (diss., Helsinki, 1997) (Theology of Paradox: Luther's Heidelberg Disputation of 1518).

16. Pekka Kärkkäinen, "Luthers trinitarische Theologie des Heiligen Geistes" (diss., Helsinki, 2003) (Luther's Trinitarian Theology of the Holy Spirit).

17. Olli-Pekka Vainio, "Luterilaisen vanhurskauttamisopin kehitys Lutherista yksimielisyyden ohjeeseen" (diss., Helsinki 2004) (The Development of the Lutheran Doctrine of Justification from Luther to the Formula of Concord).

18. Jari Jolkkonen, "Uskon ja rakkauden sakramentti: Opin ja käytännön yhteys Martti Lutherin ehtoollisteologiassa" (diss., Helsinki, 2004) (The Sacrament of Faith and Love: The Connection between Doctrine and Practice in Martin Luther's Theology of the Lord's Supper).

19. Miikka Ruokanen, "Doctrina divinitus inspirata: Martin Luther's Position in the Ecumenical Problem of Biblical Inspiration" (diss., Helsinki, 1985). Ruokanen published also a Finnish study on Luther's notion of the Bible; see Ruokanen, *Lutherin raamattukäsitys* (Tampere, 1986).

20. Kalevi Tanskanen, "Luther ja keskiajan talousetiikka: Vertaileva tutkimus" (diss., Helsinki, 1990) (Economic Ethics in Luther and in the Middle Ages).

21. Eeva Martikainen, "Oppi—metafysiikkaa vai teologiaa? Lutherin käsitys opista" (diss., Helsinki, 1987) (Doctrine—Metaphysics or Theology? Luther's Notion of Doctrine).

22. Bernice Sundkvist, "Det sakramentala draget i Luthers förkunnelse" (diss., Åbo, 2001) (The Sacramental Character of Luther's Proclamation).

23. Kaarlo Arffman, "Yliopistot ja kirkon magisterium reformaation alkuvaiheessa," vol. 1: 1517–1521 (Helsinki, 1981); vol 2: 1521–1528 (Helsinki, 1985); vol. 3: 1521–1528 (Helsinki, 1990) (The Universities and the Magisterium of the Church at the Beginning of the Reformation).

24. Arffman, *Sanan jäljet: Kirkon historian merkitys Martti Lutherin teologiassa* (Helsinki, 1993) (Tracks of the Word: The Significance of the History of the Church in Martin Luther's Theology). Arffman, *Reformaatio vai restituutio? Historiallinen argumentti reformaattoreiden ja kastajaliikkeen väittelyssä lapsikasteen oikeutuksesta* (Helsinki, 1994) (Reformation or Restitution? Historical Arguments at the Debates between the Reformers and Anabaptists about the Justification of Infant Baptism). Arffman, *Die Reformation und die Geschichte der Kirche* (Helsinki, 1997) (Reformation and the History of the Church). Also Arffman, *Mitä oli luterilaisuus? Johdatus kadonneeseen eurooppalaiseen kristinuskon tulkintaan* (Helsinki, 1996) (What was Lutheranism? Introduction to the Lost European Interpretation of the Christian Faith).

Index

(Terms and concepts such as God, Christ, love, God's Love, Human Love, and Luther occur throughout this book.)